Staff Development in
Public Welfare Agencies

Staff Development in
Public Welfare Agencies

Carol H. Meyer

COLUMBIA UNIVERSITY PRESS
New York and London, 1966

Carol H. Meyer is Associate Professor at
Columbia University School of Social Work

Copyright © 1966 by Columbia University Press
Library of Congress Catalog Card Number: 66-10730
Printed in the United States of America

Reason is not merely detached understanding;
it is conviction, fired with enthusiasm.

HOWLETT'S INTRODUCTION TO *Plato.* I. xi.

Introductory Note

This is a book about in-service training of nonprofessional public welfare staff. It aims to demonstrate a method of training designed to improve social work practice within the large bureaucratic public welfare structures of this country. Its ultimate interest is the provision of more adequate social services to the clientele of public assistance and child welfare programs.

The book is not about agency programs, nor is it primarily concerned with curriculum development in a public welfare agency. It is about public welfare staff who live and work in a world in which they must cope with inconsistent practices, rigid policies, competitive people, and contradictory values. It is a book about training within and for that world. It begins in the present, but it reaches for the future; it offers some practical ideas, but they rest on a firm philosophical commitment to social work in public welfare; it is concerned with personnel as they are and where they are, but it affirms that there are horizons of staff development yet to be reached.

The volume may find its way to social workers who are in training, and perhaps they will recognize themselves and be amused by the familiar concerns that are raised. However, it is addressed particularly to those administrators, staff trainers, and social work educators who are involved with the development of nonprofessional social welfare personnel. It is not by any means a blueprint for action; it is, rather, a framework that is applicable to agencies of many kinds, for their use in accordance with the particulars of their own programs and staff requirements.

The author has assumed a particular stance about some crucial issues that are involved in public welfare and staff development. Those issues are stated below and are developed in the first three chapters. They comprise the framework and indeed the rationale for the structure, content, and aims of the type of training program that is recommended in the subsequent chapters.

First, it is assumed that public welfare programs will continue indefinitely to be staffed primarily by nonprofessional personnel who are college graduates but not graduates of schools of social work. Moreover, the utilization of this preponderantly undergraduate group need not necessarily be a drawback to the carrying out of modern public welfare programs, as long as the nonprofessional people are perceived as social work technicians, trained for particular tasks and differing from professional social workers in their job profile, functioning, and training.

Second, in view of the fact that public welfare personnel are part of bureaucratic structures large and small, staff training cannot exist outside of that context. Thus, the form and purposes of an agency training program must observe the patterns of organization within the agency, including hierarchical arrangements of personnel, administrative controls, accountability machinery, the constraints of civil service, and the career commitments of incumbent staff. Staff training, then, must reflect the bureaucratic structure; it cannot work against the existing strains but rather must be adapted to the equilibrium of forces within the agency. The role of staff training is a limited one when conceived as affecting the agency program in fundamental ways; on the other hand, it is indispensable to the carrying out of the program.

Third, the limitations involved in agency structure and program contribute to a clear demarcation between the training of public welfare staff within the agency and the education of a professional social worker in a graduate school. It follows that the content, methods, and purposes of an agency training program will pursue an educational course that is different from that of a school curriculum.

In taking this approach the author recognizes that public assistance programs in the 1960s are in transition between two extremes of ideology. On the one hand they require a means test to some extent based upon concepts of the worthiness of the individual, and at the opposite pole they envision a total social insurance program providing economic security for all people. Service amendments to the Public Welfare Law have broadened the scope of the social worker's job, but they have not softened the effects of the indignities of the means test and the strains of excessive accountability. Therefore, this book endeavors to encompass a training program for personnel in public assistance agencies which must observe the limitations inherent in the present-day public welfare program, and at the same time achieve the end of preparing staff to meet human need wherever it is apparent.

It is difficult to know precisely just when a work such as this begins and just exactly who it was along the way who helped to develop its various themes. It is safe to say that the undertaking had its inception more than five years before the book took form, when I had the opportunity to participate in a staff development program in public welfare that was viewed then as a "demonstra-tion program." Therefore, I must gratefully acknowledge the participation of people and agencies who did not know, any more than I did, that a book would come out of the experiences we had.

The agencies and the personnel I will name are natu-rally not responsible for the contents of the book, although they can, if they wish, take credit for providing the sup-ports—financial and otherwise—that gave the training programs increased importance. Among those agencies, the United States Children's Bureau was a primary force as it responded with trust and assistance to the request of an enlightened administration of the New York City Bu-reau of Child Welfare for a new kind of staff development program. Staff members of the Bureau of Child Welfare courageously made themselves available to training ex-periments, some of which failed while others lasted.

Then, the Commissioner of Welfare and many members of the staff of the Bureau of Public Assistance became involved in an extension of the training program. It was not always smooth going, but somehow the staff and I survived each other.

There were many in the Department of Welfare who understood the modest goals of our program and who worked very hard to try to achieve them. I thank par-ticularly all those in the Harlem Welfare Center who participated, but especially the administrative staff and the supervisors who became teachers in that Center under the program.

The story of this book does not end with the experi-ment in the New York City Department of Welfare. For it really could be written only from a distance, when actual experiences could take on new meanings through broader perspectives about bureaucratic organization, so-cial work education, professionalism, and public welfare.

This distance made it possible to write a book that would have application to programs outside New York City.

During the process of preparation and writing I accumulated a series of obligations to close friends, and to colleagues at the Columbia University School of Social Work. They listened, criticized, and offered suggestions; they helped me gain the perspective that was needed to write about that intimate all-engrossing working experience.

The mechanics of preparing a book for publication sometimes seem more insuperable than managing the ideas and the writing. Without superb editing and typing assistance from secretarial staff at the Columbia University School of Social Work the ideas would still be in my head. The encouragement of the staff of Columbia University Press was not insignificant to the entire process, and the expert help of the Columbia University School of Social Work Library staff was, as always, impeccable.

To the agencies involved and to these people in particular, I am grateful beyond measure. I have not mentioned any names because that list would be too long and I think that it is best for me to take the ultimate responsibility for this book. Among those who helped me think through and experience the book's contents, not all will necessarily agree with the final outcome—but they will all know the part they played. I hope that most of them will be glad.

Contents

Foreword

by James R. Dumpson

COMMISSIONER OF WELFARE, CITY OF NEW YORK

Public welfare stands at an important crossroad in its development as the major government financed and administered social welfare program. Two crucial tasks confront public welfare administrators, their colleagues in government, and those legislators who carry the ultimate responsibility for determining whether public welfare shall effectively fulfill its mission of caring for, protecting, and contributing to the rehabilitation of people who require its services. The first of these tasks is to free public welfare from its prevalent English Poor Law mentality of contempt for the poor, by updating its policies and practices in order that its services may have meaningful relevance to current needs of people who hold a right to be recipients of them when they are in need. The second of these tasks is to make it possible for public welfare to have and to hold the number and quality of personnel it requires to fulfill its mission effectively. Indeed, these are complementary requisites for public welfare if its primary mission is, as I believe it is, to be one of our nation's essential institutions for the protection and conservation of America's human resources. Its policies, practices, stand-

ards, and the caliber of personnel who make available its
services determine whether what it offers and the manner
in which it is offered will help build and enrich human
lives and thereby contribute to the general welfare, or
whether the activities of public welfare will weaken and
erode human lives and prevent the assurance of the general welfare.

This book expertly deals with these life and death matters of public welfare and reaffirms my conviction that
training cannot be an appendage to the public welfare
agency; it cannot be a beautiful layer of ornamental professional activities to be laid aside when the pressures of
deadlines seem intolerable, when financial stringency is
the order of the day, or when public clamor for fiscal
accountability for each case is the prevailing national climate. Staff training and development are an integral part
of public welfare administration, and affect and are affected by total agency philosophy and operation. This
theme with its development is a unique contribution of
this book. Dr. Meyer outlines with clarity and professional
discipline the tasks that challenge every public welfare
administrator who takes conscientiously the tremendous
responsibility he carries for directing his agency toward
its social mission, and she emphasizes the extent to which
qualified staff determine its realization.

Dr. Meyer differentiates between the professional social
worker whose training is the responsibility of the schools
of social work, and the social work technician whose training is the responsibility of the public welfare agency.
We have long known that the full staffing of public welfare agencies by professional social workers in the foreseeable future is unrealistic. But Dr. Meyer properly urges
recognition of the value and importance of clearly identifying and differentiating the social work functions in public welfare, and recognition of those functions that quite

properly belong to the social work technician and those
that quite properly belong to the professional social
worker. Staff training and development within this formulation emerge as a social work process and are an in-
escapable responsibility of the public welfare agency.
This clarity about the training staff function in public
welfare and the resultant training process holds immeas-
urable promise to the immediate improvement of public
welfare. That improvement will be facilitated and ac-
celerated if the social work profession not only heeds the
author's plea that it acknowledge that some social services
can be administered by the social work technician, but
also that the profession meet its obligation to accept the
social work technician within its fold and assume its responsibility of helping improve the technician's practice.
In no small way the public image of social work and the
public's future support of it depends on its image of
public welfare.

Of immediate interest to schools of social work will be
Dr. Meyer's clear delineation of their role in training for
public welfare. It seems to me that in greatly enlarged
areas of collaboration, public welfare agencies and schools
of social work, financially aided by all levels of government, will move ahead within this formulation as
partners recognizing their separate and distinctive roles.
As a result we in public welfare will be able to make one
important choice concerning the direction public welfare
should and can take as it faces its crossroads in present-
day and future development.

Written out of experience and based on an unassailable
theoretical foundation, this is a book especially for every
public welfare administrator in the United States. But it
is also a book written for the dean of every school of
social work who is committed to strengthening practices
in public welfare. It is written no less for every local, state,

and federal legislator who, in the final analysis, will determine the way public welfare will go and the extent to which a government program may help people out of poverty and deprivation. And because no administrator of public welfare and no legislator can function effectively for the public good without the aid, support, and critical guidance of informed, concerned lay leaders in the field of social welfare, Dr. Meyer's book will add to the understanding and, I hope, encouragement for even more support and critical guidance of that respected and increasingly larger group of men and women who want the best for all people and who believe public welfare can be one of the instruments for achieving it.

The New York City Department of Welfare, its staff, and its Commissioner are proud and inspired to have had a part in that particular professional journey of Dr. Meyer that finally led to this book.

New York, N.Y.
July, 1965

Staff Development in
Public Welfare Agencies

Chapter One

Of People There Are Plenty

In this period of rapidly developing social and economic welfare programs in the United States, an extreme shortage of competent social welfare staff threatens to negate the effectiveness of those programs. The public welfare service amendments of 1956 and 1962 mandated that social services were to become integrated with public assistance, and that prevention of social breakdown and rehabilitation were to be part of all case planning. The enrichment of public welfare thus envisioned requires that agencies employ knowledgeable, effective social service staff in order to realize the new service goals. The number of staff involved could reach as high as 80,000—a small army of personnel to be prepared for new tasks. New recruits must be trained. Moreover, all evidence points to the conclusion that people presently on staff cannot be spared from the jobs they are doing, while at the same time they must learn to carry out new functions.

The question of how huge numbers of personnel can be trained effectively for an increasing number of jobs and improved quality of functioning in social welfare programs has been explored by many groups and individuals in public and private welfare agencies, national social welfare organizations, and schools of social work. In particular, the efforts of the Division of Technical Training in the Bureau of Family Services and the United States Children's Bureau of the Department of Health, Education, and Welfare, the American Public Welfare Association, and state and local training departments in public welfare agencies must be acknowledged. Those groups have foreseen the manpower crisis and have struggled for years to develop and raise practice standards in public welfare programs. The field of staff training has become a familiar subject of articles in professional and technical journals, and a common subject of concern as responsible citizens and social workers are slowly coming to recognize the strange paradox of the 1960s. In this country, government has turned one-quarter of its economic resources toward improvement of the public's welfare. Through legislation it has provided for the widest variety of social services for people in need, but, oddly, there is such a deficiency in supply of personnel skilled enough to allocate those services wisely, that in actual practice the agencies have been unable to make full use of the broad public welfare services now available.

In the United States it is not uncommon to equate lack of professionally trained social workers with a shortage of personnel, yet this is not a precise definition of the manpower shortage. Obviously, there are sufficient people at large in this country who might be called upon to serve in public and private social agencies. However, limitations in training facilities and absence of social work skills, combined with a certain unreadiness to utilize permanently a force of nonprofessional social workers, contribute to the notion that there is a serious personnel shortage. It is a well-documented fact that there is a lack of a professionally educated reservoir of personnel, and this condition will undoubtedly continue for many years to come. Yet, despite statistical evidence to the contrary, the ideal persists that all social welfare personnel should be professionally educated in order to carry out the service programs in public welfare. Since it has become apparent that it may be impossible to achieve this ideal, compromises have been made and distortions have occurred which have led social welfare planners, administrators, and educators to view personnel as being in various stages of preprofessionalism and semiprofessionalism; it has been difficult for the field to face the fact that a large majority of personnel will remain nonprofessional social workers.

An illustration of the prevailing unwillingness or inability to come to terms with the inevitability that nonprofessional social service staff are a permanent working force in public welfare, may be observed in the role that graduate schools of social work are called upon to play. It is recognized that those schools are unable to educate a sufficient number of professional personnel having two years of full-time residence as the accepted school experience. In view of this fact, varieties of alternative plans are often suggested by the field at large, and at times even recommended by the schools themselves. Some of the plans suggest that students attend school for one year, or that they participate in a nonresidence program as part-time students. Other adaptations are offered as well—for example, that students attend without participating in field work, or that they meet this requirement by remaining on their jobs and getting field work credit for this semi-educational experience. Out of the pressure to establish a level of quasi-professionalism, there is some danger that the educational experience which creates a professional social worker will be impaired, and his preparation for effective social service seriously undermined.

Another illustration of the field's insistence upon treating most social work personnel as potentially professional, even though the statistical evidence suggests a contrary condition, is the common view that nongraduate staff members are practicing on a *pre*professional level, expecting sooner or later to become graduates. There seems to be less emphasis upon delineating jobs that can be done appropriately by a permanent group of nonprofessionals than there is upon moving those people on into graduate schools. Naturally, at times in individual instances postgraduate work is a reasonable aim that can be achieved. However, in planning for effective utilization of available personnel on the broad scene of social welfare, it is not entirely realistic to assume that all or most social welfare personnel will ever attend graduate schools of social work full time to achieve a master's degree.

Given this dilemma—that professional social work staffing is desirable to such a degree that any worker with less than full qualifications is viewed as "not yet" professional, and the opposing condition that schools of social work undoubtedly will be unable to meet the increasing demand for professionally educated social workers—an adjustment must be made. Either the schools will have to modify their programs, provide a shorter educational experience, and expand numerically far beyond their present limits, or the field will have to revise its conception of the jobs to be done so as to utilize more effectively the personnel who are available.

If professional workers are not now and are not likely to become available in sufficient numbers, it may be fruitful to assume a different stance in assessing the problem and its possible solution. What then? In this book we submit a here-and-now proposal for the development of staff on the job, within the public welfare agency. Our plan rests upon the existence of certain conditions—that there will be a clear definition of the functions and tasks of all social workers in public welfare, professional as well as nonprofessional, and that there will be supports reflected in the administrative practices of the agency for the staff development program. The staff to be trained within the agency would not be perceived as preprofessional social workers, but would occupy a career line as social work technicians.

Recommendations along these lines are to be found in Dael Wolfle's excellent survey on human resources, in which he speaks of better utilization of available personnel.[1] Kahn,[2] Wolfe,[3] and Buell[4] in the field of social welfare have suggested this approach as the primary way to handle the personnel shortage realistically. Whether jobs in social welfare programs are to be defined by their complexity or simplicity, by case categorization, by worker classification, or by functional determinants, the issue here is that somehow public welfare functions must be examined and broken down into identifiable parts so that tasks may be accomplished by personnel who are not and probably never will be professionally educated in schools of social work. Wolfle says that ". . . systematic training of assistants has not been extensively developed outside of the medical fields . . . ,"[5] and this is certainly true in the field of social welfare. This is not to say that most social agencies do not use nonprofessional staff; rather that the agencies and the profession have not yet accepted this expedient measure as a permanent device. Thus, the use of technical staff has not been systematized, much less assimilated as an integral part of social work practice.

Personnel—Supply and Demand

There is startling factual evidence of the imbalance of supply and demand in staff resources in social welfare. The problem can be examined from several angles—the availability of appropriate personnel in the total job market, the particular requirements of selection and recruitment efforts, the potential of professional education for provision of staff, and the utilization of personnel. These are viewed as separate issues for purposes of discussion, but in the long run they are interrelated. When all aspects of lack of personnel are juxtaposed to the varied and increasing demands, it can be seen that the staff shortage requires that serious measures be taken on all levels to accommodate welfare operations to this major problem.

Looking first at the picture of total resources of potential social workers, one need only note the increased birth rate in the United States during and after World War II, and the present rise in the number of high school and college graduates.[6] The United States Department of Labor [7] predicts a 43 percent increase in the number of professional and technical workers between 1960 and 1970, from 7.5 million in 1960 to 10.7 million in 1970. The number in 1970 will account for 13.3 percent of the total labor force, compared with 11.2 percent ten years earlier. This will of course be the result of an increase in high school and college educated people, both absolutely and in proportion to the population. It is as yet undetermined how adequate the future supply will be when it is allocated among occupations, but in the light of the advancement of automation and technical unemployment, there will be increasing opportunities for the as yet unautomated service professions to attract educated young people, even though many people with educational backgrounds will be needed by private industry. Furthermore, if these human resources should be depleted, the service professions might well examine the statistics that describe the rising number of educated people in early retirement and the upsurge of educated women who are moving steadily into the employment market. Leaving aside for the moment the specific refinements involving selection, recruitment, and training of potential social workers from these ranks, one can see from human statistics alone that in this country there is clearly no lack of resources as far as people are concerned. The country's manpower problem, it is generally agreed, is more related to quality and utilization than to numbers.

However, it is not enough to know that potential personnel exists for the asking. Obviously, a young college graduate who might have been interested in factory management would not necessarily translate that interest to social work even if he could not break into the factory management field. To a large extent the choice of vocation or profession is a personal one, governed largely by elusive factors such as interest, educational choices, family background, cultural determinants, attitudes, and self-image, as well as by the more measurable components of aptitudes, skills, and opportunities. Thus, recruitment and selection efforts must be geared to particular kinds of young people, retired people, or housewives.

What kinds of people? It is difficult to know with certainty the specific characteristics of good potential staff. This lack of concreteness is due partly to uncertain criteria and partly to the lack of formalized study of personnel requirements both for professional schools and for social work jobs at large.

For one thing, a particular school or agency would not be able always to state accurately the qualities regarded highly in a student or a staff member; moreover, in a diminishing student or labor market, admissions or job requirements are often modified. The fact is that criteria are subjective and often conflicting, as each school and agency defines its own standards in accordance with its specific cultural orientation and requirements.

A second reason for the lack of criteria is that the job to be done in social work is not always defined clearly or understood in the community as a whole. While individual social workers, agencies, and schools can describe the functions and tasks of the social worker in many particulars, it would be difficult for a given cross section to formulate a composite picture that would give support to nationwide recruitment efforts.

One of the questions that must be answered before seeking personnel from the increasing number of people who will be available to work in social welfare programs is whether recruitment is to be for jobs in particular social agencies, or for the profession and thus for schools of social work. There is a difference. The chief requirement of an agency seeking to hire a staff member is that he must be able to do the job. If the agency has differentiated professional from nonprofessional tasks and functions, the direction of its recruitment efforts will be self-evident; for the professional function it will turn only to the supply of graduates of schools of social work, and for the nonprofessional tasks it will broaden its scope of hiring and turn to the total supply of college graduates who are not committed to other jobs and professions.

In the last several decades, when it became apparent that the demand for professionally educated social workers was far outreaching the supply, both voluntary and government agencies began to devise ways of coping with the situation. The most common way in extensive use by the mid-sixties was to hire nonprofessional personnel, as well as graduate social workers when they could be found, in order to carry out the service program of the agency, but with the intention of sending those without graduate degrees to professional schools as soon as they could be spared. Thus, there has been a proliferation of work-study programs, where staff has been, in a sense, loaned to professional education, hopefully to be returned in two years to serve out at least a commitment of one or two years in the agency's service.

In our exploration of the complexities of the personnel problem, it is essential at this early stage to consider the implications of this form of recruitment and hiring. It suggests that the agencies consider the workers in question as preprofessional; in other words, as potential graduate students. Actually, this may or may not be so in individual instances. The ability to carry out some jobs effectively in a social agency may not necessarily correlate with the educational demands of a professional school. (A recent study on admissions showed that among 2,466 applicants who were not accepted in schools of social work, 40.24 percent were academically ineligible and 34.46 percent had personal qualities that made them unsuited for social work education.) [8] The selection and recruitment efforts carried on by schools of social work are geared primarily to the qualification that the applicant be a good potential student, and the nonprofessional staff member who may be giving impeccable service in a social agency may not necessarily be student material for any number of reasons, including the fact that he may not be interested in academic pursuits.

Of more serious import is the implication that the field of social work, in its efforts to recruit preprofessional and professional staff as a solution to manpower shortages, has not come to terms with the fact that as recently as 1960 only 18 percent of all direct service personnel in government and voluntary agencies held graduate social work degrees, and that this was only a 5 percent increase over a ten-year period. In state and local government agencies alone 10 percent of all direct service workers were social work graduates, an increase of 4 percent in ten years. [9] In the shadow of these statistics the field of social work has yet to accept the fact that 82 percent of the direct service practitioners are not professional or preprofessional at all, but are serving as nonprofessional staff.

If the low numbers of graduates on staff in all agencies (which totaled about 25,000 in 1965) [10] and the slow rate of increase in ten years is not sufficiently impressive, let us look at the potential in the area of professional education as a source of supply of graduate staff, in order to examine how realistic the plan for complete professionalization of staff is.

The slow rate of expansion of existing educational resources can be judged by comparing the total number in the graduating classes of schools of social work in 1954 and 1963. In 1954 there were 1,651 graduates from 52 schools, and in 1963 there were 2,678 from 58 schools, a difference of only 1,027.[11] The capacity of the nation's professional social work schools has been estimated to be about 6,100 to 7,100 full-time students enrolled in both years of school,[12] which means that less than half this number will be graduated each year.

A consideration of the estimated need of professional staff should be possible so as to assess the extent to which the number of about 3,000 graduates a year will meet the estimated needs of the field at large. Actually, this assessment is not possible for the total field of social welfare, as firm statistical estimates are not available in all areas of practice.[13] Projections for public welfare, however, are available. In public welfare in 1961 a national estimate was made of staff needs in public assistance.[14] In 1960 social service staff numbered 34,887, of whom 1,608 or 4.6 percent had had two years or more of professional education. The estimate suggested for 1970 was for a total of 66,850 social service personnel in public assistance, to include a component of 22,400—or 33 per cent—graduate workers.

In public child welfare the staffing situation is serious but not quite to the same degree as in public assistance.

The number of personnel involved is not as large, and the proportion of professionally trained staff has always been greater in child welfare. In 1958, when there were 6,452 on total child welfare staff, 1,807 or 28 percent were professionally trained. At that time it was estimated that 13,770 fully trained public child welfare workers would be needed in 1970, indicating a need for 11,963 more than in 1958.[15] The situation changed markedly in child welfare in five years as service was expanded, and in 1963 there were 9,348 social service staff positions in public child welfare,[16] which included a proportionally larger number of those professionally trained.

On balance, then, the total number of professionally trained staff needed in 1970 in public welfare alone has been estimated to be approximately 36,000. The source of recruits—the 3,000 to 3,500 graduates a year from schools of social work—must be shared with other fields of practice, which are also expanding under government and voluntary auspices.

In the first place, public welfare programs utilized only 51 percent of all social workers, trained and untrained, in 1960.[17] While this percentage might well increase by 1970, public welfare personnel surely will not constitute the total number of social welfare personnel. Because of the general demand, even the source of supply of staff to be trained will not be unlimited.

More to the point is the fact that the percentage of professionally trained social workers in 1960 who were working in public welfare accounted for only 22 percent of all trained workers, and according to one estimate [18] only 12 percent were employed in direct service jobs. While it can be assumed that public welfare will be reaping the benefits of increased educational leave programs, and that by 1970 a larger proportion of graduates will be working in public assistance and child welfare programs, the potential source of supply of graduates must be examined in order to assess the reasonableness of the estimate of 36,000 professionals in public welfare by 1970.

At the rate of 3,000 graduates a year, the number that might be accumulated between 1960 and 1970 is 30,000. If public welfare programs were to attract as many as 10 percent more from trained resources by 1970 than they did in 1960, or 32 percent of the total graduates, the number would still amount to only 9,600 new professional staff. Accounting for the fact that in 1960 there were about 3,500 professional staff in public welfare, and not allowing for resignations and retirement, an additional number approximating 23,000 would be needed by 1970. Given a hypothetically stable situation, where estimates of graduates and potential staff needs did not change radically, and where other social welfare programs made consistent demands upon the supply of graduates, it would take almost 40 years for public welfare to achieve its estimated goal of 36,000 professionally trained social workers.

The demand for professional staff in public welfare has increased due to the states' efforts to implement the public welfare amendments, and is a reflection of the expanded definition of need as expressed in those amendments. But the question of staff turnover must also be included in our deliberation of the general manpower problem, for we must be as concerned with continuity and retention as we are with recruitment. According to one estimate [19] the rate of turnover of caseworkers in public child welfare agencies in 1957 was 20 percent. In public assistance agencies in 1963 the average rate nationally was 26 percent per annum.[20] Thus, it is evident that the accession or hiring rate must be greater than 20–26 percent of the present staff in order merely to replace those who have separated from the public agencies for one reason or another.

What of the states' efforts to train staff through educational leave programs? There have been gains, of course, but in the light of the limited potential of schools of social work for educating a large number of students, leave programs can result in only a slight reduction in professional personnel shortages. At the end of the academic year in June 1963, 914 child welfare workers and 1,038 public assistance workers were attending graduate schools of social work full time.[21] While this is a good number of people, at this rate graduates would hardly supply the estimated need. Public welfare agencies cannot spare staff, scholarship assistance is not uniformly adequate, not all states take advantage of the federal policy of matching full salary and educational costs, and, perhaps most significantly, public welfare jobs are not sufficiently equated with the professional skill and knowledge of the returning graduates, who may then leave for other jobs.

In the light of the limited educational opportunities in graduate schools, competition with other public agencies and voluntary agencies for available professional staff, and the fact that public welfare jobs are not as yet generally adapted to the level of professional competence, it is unlikely that we can look for any marked change in the professional profile of public welfare staff in the very near future.

Suggested Solutions

Since 1961, when the United States Department of Labor and the Department of Health, Education, and Welfare, together with the National Social Welfare Assembly, published the now famous *Manpower Study,* the facts of the manpower situation in social welfare have been known. The suggested solutions to the problem are varied and, when seen together, often contradictory. A common recommendation is that the schools of social work must expand in order to meet the need for staff. While this is a reasonable expectation, we have already touched upon its inadequacy as a major solution. Even if the number of graduates could be raised 100 percent, it would still take 20 years to provide sufficient personnel to meet current estimations of staffing needs in public welfare. In a later chapter on professional education we shall deal with some of the components of social work education itself and with the financial, space, and faculty restrictions that will inevitably limit this recommendation as a realistic solution to the total manpower deficiency.

Alternatives that have to do with various forms of nonprofessional training as substitute measures for professional education have been suggested. We should note the key word here: substitute. In the search for solutions to the problem of shortages of personnel, it seems that professional education is often the sacrificial lamb when all else fails.

One suggestion is that since graduate schools of social work cannot or will not expand their facilities, then technical institutes to train nonprofessional personnel can be developed to do the job.[22] To do it as well? Or better? It is very unlikely that they could. Because the education of professional social workers requires interdisciplinary facilities, that education has been proven to be best advanced in schools of social work affiliated with universities. For this reason, other types of training facilities would be less than adequate to the task. In a recent publication on technical training it was pointed out that:

American educational thought strongly resists the development of separate schools, and offers important status and support only to the more comprehensive institution within one educational mainstream . . . demonstrably, no form of American education has successfully risen in importance outside the main structure of education.[23]

Moreover, there is some question that technical institutes for social work training would find acceptance in this country. It has been noted paradoxically that:

. . . the absence of status and prestige for vocational and technical education has its roots in two American values. The first is the traditional ideal of preventing class distinctions within our society. The second is the status of the baccalaureate and advanced degrees as a hallmark of social achievement and distinction.[24]

Perhaps it would be more accurate to describe such proposed training institutes as different in aim and educational method, much as the training of one-year graduates would be different from the training of two-year graduates. The governing principle here is that we cannot expect the same results from dissimilar approaches, and that different approaches do not become the same simply by being called by similar names. In this same vein it is often suggested that graduate schools should provide for part-time learning, usually classroom instruction without student field work practice, so that staff may continue to work in the agencies while attending school.

Among other limitations that might be foreseen in the establishment of technical training institutes to an extent sufficient to fill the personnel gap in social agencies, is the inevitable competition with professional schools of social work for qualified teaching staff. Is this not, then, proliferating the problem of uneconomical deployment of personnel?

Keeping in mind that the aim of nonprofessional training programs is to develop skills for practice in agencies, we might well ask which agencies the institutes would train for, and whether specific training aims could actually be met outside the agencies themselves. All agencies have different programs, policies, and procedures, and usually the tasks and functions assigned to social workers are allotted in particular ways. Agencies would still have to train their technical staff for the work to be done, much as they must train graduate professional staff for their specific jobs. Thus, social work training schools would not be strictly academic institutions, nor would they be quite identical with the job setting into which the technician would move.

For all these reasons, therefore, whether or not technical institutes for social work training develop in this country, we cannot predict that they would serve the purpose of meeting the manpower shortage in such a way that social work skills would be taught to sufficient numbers of personnel to man the complex social service programs in public and private agencies.

Despite the complexities of the problem, the imbalance between supply and demand of professional personnel, the present mandates to provide services notwithstanding the unavailability of adequate staff, and the pressing needs of public welfare clients, a solution must be found to the existing situation. When conditions are confronted squarely, it is not productive to set our sights upon full professional education for all social workers in public welfare. Nor does it appear to be of value to agency practice and professional social work to develop so-called semiprofessional institutes of training which would neither orient personnel to specific agency practices nor increase the supply of graduate social workers. There is a third approach, one which this book will consider in some depth: a program of in-service training, developed within each public welfare agency for its own staff.[25] In this connection, staff is defined as all personnel—administrative, supervisory, practitioner, and clerical. This definition of staff includes as well the graduate social worker who has been inducted into the profession, but who at any stage of his career may elect to work in a public welfare agency and will need orientation to its practices, as well as continuing opportunities to improve his skills and increase his knowledge. The nongraduate technician will, of course, need identical in-service training opportunities, even though the content of his learning like that of the clerical worker will be on a different plane.

Viewing the goals of in-service training in this way does not imply a substitution for professional education. A clear distinction between professional education and agency training will, in the long run, be helpful to the task of realistically dealing with the impact of the professional manpower shortage.

The concept of staff development with which this book is concerned has been expressed in the following statement:

Staff development is a function of the administration of the agency, not a separate field of practice or an agency-centered school program. When perceived thus, a program of staff development grows out of and is conditioned by staff learning needs and administrative readiness to meet these needs. The chief goal is improvement in the practice of agency staff.[26]

Chapter Two

Public Welfare—Strains and Stresses

The vast scope of public welfare programs and the severe lack of adequately trained personnel available to carry out those programs have placed overwhelming demands upon the public agencies and their total complement of staff. State plans have been submitted before training personnel are available, training programs have been hastily developed to meet current pressures, and throughout the country there is great unevenness in the provision of ongoing in-service training for all public welfare staff.

When a problem of such magnitude confronts us, usually we do what we can or must to adapt to the immediate situation, and we consider later the theory underlying our actions. When "later" arrives it is often too late, for we have by then arranged our programs in some fashion, and in short order they have become traditional. Training directors have been hired, materials mimeographed, space allocated, and staff introduced to new ways of practicing; soon it seems to be too late to accommodate even a relatively new program to a theoretical model.

In the light of bureaucratic complexities and multiple requirements on many levels, it is not too surprising that the idea of in-service training is often oversimplified in order to enable us to grasp its total concept. It is often misconstrued as a *unilateral* device to enable social work staff to carry out their jobs skillfully and efficiently. Most often in-service training is superimposed upon existing programs, much as if it were a new service to be offered by the agency, inserted almost surreptitiously into an ongoing administrative structure without awareness or participation on the part of the staff itself.

In-service training is infinitely more complex than that; it is inextricably involved with all aspects of practice, the direct practice of staff, the indirect staff services that support practice, and the total administration of the agency. Staff practice is the ultimate expression of an agency's program, and the unique vehicle through which clients receive public assistance and social services. It is the major connection between administrative direction and the carrying out of the purposes of the agency—the way in which the legal mandates and attitudes of the community get translated into action. It is our thesis that staff development, viewed as a process that affects every aspect of the agency's work, is characterized by its mobility, in that it may be concerned with all kinds and levels of staff and with the entire range of practice strategies in the agency. It carries an administrative and educative function which, when based upon social work concepts, values, and principles, can be viewed as a social work process. By definition this suggests a continuous movement, an ongoing program that has little to do with restrictions of time, place, or status. Particularly within a bureaucratic structure where just these restrictions become too easily solidified, it is useful to view the staff development process as an integral part of the life of a public welfare agency, not an appendage to any of its parts.

Thus, it is important first to explore the complexities surrounding staff practice, the interweaving forces that affect its direction and impinge upon its quality. For it is only as this context is understood that one can know the purpose of developing staff, the aims to be sought in training, and the ways in which tasks must be carried out. After one examines the interacting components of the systems surrounding staff practice, it is easier to recognize that staff development must permeate an agency and be more than an additional program. The significant systems are those that have to do with organizational factors and the community within which the agency exists.

As it is described by Vinter, "The agency is conceived of as internally organized, having a distinctive structure with interdependent components and functioning in a social environment." [1] In the surrounding complex that staff practice reflects, each thread contains its own characteristics and history, its own relationships with other significant forces. If we but had a transactional lens to examine these integral threads it would be easier to keep in mind the total effect they have upon the practice of staff, and thus the nature and direction that a staff development program should pursue.

The first "system" to which we will direct attention is the organizational system reflected in the state, county, or local public welfare department or administrative unit. Whatever the size of the agency as far as numbers of cases or personnel are concerned, whether it is an urban or rural agency, whether the staff are fully trained or not trained at all, the organization is always complex.

One of the major factors contributing to the intricacy of the organizational picture is the hierarchical arrangement of the lines of administrative responsibility. Each level of government is answerable ultimately to the next higher governmental unit, and finally to the Department of Health, Education, and Welfare and the Congress of the United States. Another factor has to do with the nature of the programs that each of these units must encompass. The number and variety are such as to require that staff practice has to be concerned with differences in demands, multilateral levels of service, and unequal, interwoven groups of tasks. Consider, for example, the fact that in varying administrative forms public assistance and child welfare programs share in the public welfare organization, and within each of these programs there is a growing list of categories of services, too often discrete from one another. Even a small agency must provide the entire spectrum of services for the public.

Not only is this system internally complex, but it also interacts with external systems which are themselves complex from any perspective. In addition to the hierarchical relationship mentioned above, the public welfare unit, and thus its staff, must be related to the community in which it operates. This includes not only the objective laws and physical attributes of the community, but also those abstract, attitudinal factors that sometimes exert more influence upon staff practice than concrete expectations. In addition to legislative limits and supports, there are such things as the social and economic systems of the nation at large; matters of job opportunities, unemployment, job displacement through automation, availability of housing, civil rights, educational facilities, and the general community attitudes toward public welfare and its recipients. All these impinge upon the level and quality of staff practice within any public welfare unit.

The third large system interacting with staff practice in public welfare agencies may be described as the welfare establishment at large. This includes other public and private agencies—probation, parole, and family court services, public school social work, mental health, psychiatric and medical health services, as well as private family and child welfare services. Whether these social agency services are seen as supplementary to or conflicting with some public welfare services, or whether we look only at the referral process among agencies, it is evident that the staff in public welfare agencies carry the burden of the welfare program when it is effective and indeed when it is restrictive for clients. The image of the workers in public welfare carried by their social work colleagues in other agencies will inevitably affect the morale and self-perception of public welfare personnel, and thus their practice. Sometimes the public welfare worker is held accountable for all of the lacks in services, and not always is he credited with achievement in effectively utilizing the services that are available.

The fourth large system with which the unit of public welfare interacts is the interrelated educational and professional system which helps to define the direction public welfare staff take in their practice. In most communities in the United States social workers in public welfare departments are recruited from undergraduate colleges, although there are still a number of local and county public welfare agencies which draw staff from high school graduates. As the staff are preponderantly college graduates, there is a close relationship between the undergraduate curriculum and the new staff member. The Council on Social Work Education Curriculum Study [2] explored the issues involved in the preparation of undergraduates for employment in public welfare agencies, and concluded that students could be so prepared through an enrichment of the curriculum to include a concentration on social science subjects and elementary social work principles. There is evidence to suggest that a great deal of work is being done in undergraduate schools to provide college graduates with the necessary background for work in public welfare.[3] From the point of view of staff practice in public welfare it is desirable to know how to think, to make judgments, to take limited responsibility, to collect and assess facts about people and their social and economic situations. How this preparation is accomplished in the undergraduate school is not as vital to our thesis as the fact that it be accomplished. We will, therefore, not deal further with this educational relationship in this book. The relevant point is that there is a necessary connection between the undergraduate college and public welfare which must be recognized as long as public welfare staff is to be drawn from that source.

Another segment of the educational system most directly, although not most often, related to public welfare is the graduate school of social work. Since it is the graduate school which inducts one into the profession, discussion of its role will be taken up more fully in Chapter Three.

From this glimpse of the larger systems which interact

with the public welfare system, it is apparent that staff practice cannot be isolated from the intricate components of the world immediately surrounding it. The relevant world, in the case of public welfare staff, is the public welfare hierarchical system, community attitudes, the surrounding public and private social welfare system, and at least two educational systems, one of which, the graduate school, is interwoven with the profession of social work.

In the absence of a lens powerful enough to bring into simultaneous focus all of these dynamic, interacting influences on practice, it is necessary to select particular aspects of the problem for analysis of staff development implications. We will direct attention first on the internal system of public welfare, the immediate, interacting components within the organization itself that have significance for our understanding of staff practice and staff development. To begin with, it is important to examine the aspects of agency programs that directly affect staff practice; then, particular elements of administrative controls and personnel practices that are the bedrock from which staff practice springs. Finally, the complexity of the programs and the chaotic effect of multiple characteristics and qualifications of staff lead to concern with functions and tasks, and the ways in which they are or may be allocated within the agency program.

Public Welfare—the Agency Program

American public welfare programs, responding as they must to legal mandate and community pressure, are characteristically called upon to take immediate action to comply with a multitude of requirements. There never seems to be time to think first about the introduction of a new service program—for example, to contemplate the best administrative location, to hire and train the staff before the program is in full operation, to devise an evaluation scheme at once, or, often, even to have office supplies available. Sometimes new laws, such as the 1962 amendments, are passed with no reference to the fact that as modifications of the existing welfare program they might actually set up contradictory require- ments of staff in dealing with clients. Among many knowl- edgeable critics of the current public welfare system is Professor Eveline Burns, who has commented upon "The repugnant nature of our present public assistance system . . ." and said that:

The budgetary deficiency approach with its detailed exami- nation of an individual's resources and equally detailed work- ing out of the family's itemized minimum requirements has been unchallenged for far too long. Indeed it is so offensive a procedure that we argue that such a program should be ad- ministered by highly trained social workers who are given the hopeless task of trying to make palatable something that is inherently destructive of an individual's self-esteem and privacy.[4]

Under the law, a social worker in public assistance may be asked to provide supportive casework services to a family in order to sustain the parents and children as a functioning unit in the community. The father may be unemployed and without job skills, but there may be no job retraining program in the community. His wife may be employable as a seamstress, but there may be no day care facilities for her children while she is working. This family's reliance upon public assistance requires that they continually prove their need and submit to the extreme degree of surveillance usually exercised by the social worker. That same social worker may be attempting to free them to make fuller use of their energies and potentialities. One can begin to perceive that the conflicting demands upon the worker to rehabilitate the family and also to follow procedures that promote dependency exist simultaneously. What, then, will we train that social worker for?

Another common case example of the built-in contradictions of our present public welfare system as they impinge upon staff practice is that of an adolescent boy who is being helped by the child welfare worker to achieve independent living. If this boy lives with his family he may have to turn over the bulk of his earnings to them as he begins to work. What, then, is the content of the social worker's training to be—casework or the art of bill collecting? Can the social worker be trained to sustain children in school to reduce the dropout rate when their earnings may be needed to help the family back to financial independence, which is the expressed aim of the Public Welfare Law? What is to be the nature of the social worker's training when he is again caught between two social imperatives in the case of a young mother of three children who wishes to pursue the most socially acceptable goal of staying at home and mothering her young children, while at the same time her public assistance grant is so low that she cannot afford to carry out her role at home and must meet the conflicting social demand that she go to work and become independent?

These are typical instances where conflicting demands are made upon the client and his social worker in a public welfare agency. The usual approach in social work to the resolution of a conflict where there are equal alternative pulls is to help the client know the course of action he wants and is able to follow, to strengthen him to pursue that action, and to arrange things so that he may. However, the inevitable legal and community restrictions that are as much a part of public welfare as are the opportunities within it for fulfillment, often may predetermine a case solution according to a policy or procedure rather than according to the overriding concerns, needs, capacities, and opportunities of the client.

Given this system of public welfare, most public agencies have conducted working programs through the years while coping with restrictive grants, archaic attitudes, and unrealistic mandates that have affected an ever increasing and complex kind of clientele. Whether we view the programs as expedient or imaginative is not too important; what is significant is that public welfare has in fact provided necessary financial assistance and family and child welfare services to millions of American people since 1935. It has never been possible to wait for the millennium in community support and resources, or in professional staff or tested techniques. Public welfare agencies have pushed on despite the conflicting pulls of taxpayers, lawmakers, social workers, and, of course, clients. In many communities, particularly on the eastern seaboard, local public welfare agencies are housed in the oldest public buildings and must manage with inadequate equipment and a tired and hopeless staff. They have suffered criticism from newspapers and politicians who have not meant well. Public welfare reflects many contradictions. It is a social work program that graduate professional social workers avoid; it is a government civil service program that is separate from other government programs in that it requires social work expertise; it spends a large share of federal, state, and municipal budgets and, perhaps in reverse proportion, is only tolerated by the taxpayer; it provides essential services to its clients and is often detested by the very people it serves.

It seems to be the American way to confront an imperfect system by dreaming about ways to make it perfect. While such dreams might become reality in a better future, it is nonetheless our burden to carry on with the system we have today. We are not without solutions to the terrible public welfare situation of the sixties, but these answers are in the minds and writings of our social welfare leaders, who are in fact articulate and courageous; they are not identical with the solutions sought by powerful politicians, the National Association of Manufacturers, the American Medical Association, large newspaper chains, or even the unknowing public. Let us, therefore, restate the problem and examine some solutions that represent the gamut of opinion in this country.

Public welfare programs have become increasingly significant in the lives of the 20 percent of our population who are poverty stricken, the 4 to 5 percent who are technically unemployed, and the increasing number who require public assistance. For example, in December 1963, per 1,000 of the population in the respective age groups, 123 aged 65 and over received Old Age Assistance, 12.8 aged 65 and over received Medical Assistance for the Aged, 4.7 aged 18–64 received Aid to the Permanently and Totally Disabled, 42 children under 18 received Aid to Families with Dependent Children, and 5.4 under age 65 received general assistance. Recipients of aid to the blind numbered 81 per 100,000 aged 18 and over. In addition, children receiving child welfare services from state and local public welfare agencies numbered 457,300, or 60 per 10,000 of the child population [5] Public assistance expenditure accounts for 9 percent of the gross national product in this country.[6]

In this urban, industrial society, where the extended family no longer exists to care for its own, and where daily living has become too complex for any family to be self-sufficient and completely independent of government services, social welfare programs have developed in response to residual needs that are not completely met by personal, private, or institutional systems. The economically disadvantaged group we have just cited is most often the clientele of the public welfare service program. As this group grows, as its social problems appear increasingly complex, and as the government recognizes its needs and provides the resources to meet those needs, the scope and breadth of the public welfare program are growing proportionally. And with them grows the need for skilled staff, trained to provide the services and to meet mass needs in individualized ways.

In the 1964 Roundtable Discussions of the American Public Welfare Association (APWA) it was clearly stated that "There have been few exceptions, but for the most part Public Assistance in the various states in the 1960's has been geared to perform the same function it performed in the 1930's." [7] Considering the historical events and drastic social and cultural changes that have taken place in this country and throughout the world in the last quarter of a century, it is a phenomenon of our lives and a testimony to our commitment to puritan ideals that this social institution has changed so little; that it has been so maladaptive in such radically changing times. It will be recalled that during the Depression of the 1930s, when public assistance was introduced, many of those in need of jobs were middle-class, educated, and skilled in some endeavor. The major social and economic problem for them was the unavailability of jobs. With the postwar improvement in the economy and the ensuing prosperity during and after World War II, those people were able to work and relied less upon public assistance. The program as it was conceived no longer applied to those who were, or would have been, self-directing had jobs been available to them during the Depression. Another difference in the clientele toward whom public assistance programs were directed was that many of the aged, widows, and dependent children formerly assisted through public welfare programs became eligible for Social Security or Old-Age and Survivors Insurance (OASI) benefits after 1937.

In a sense, it might be said that the citizens for whom public assistance programs were devised are no longer the primary recipients. In the 1960s, not a depression period, the clientele of public assistance programs are largely those whose total existence has been affected by a lifetime of poverty, so that economic assistance is but one of the services they require.

Today much effort is being brought to bear upon the subject of technical unemployment due to automation. The present Manpower Development and Training Act is directed toward retraining the unemployed who can be introduced into a new kind of labor market. However, it is doubtful that even this program of education and development will greatly affect the clientele of public welfare programs. A recent APWA meeting on automation was concerned with this question. Cogent arguments in support of the notion of residual characteristics of the public welfare client group were presented, and it was stated that:

The great majority of persons receiving public assistance have not had, and will not have, their need for economic support affected by automation. These recipients are not able to share in economically productive life—the aged, the blind, the severely disabled, the mothers with young children. A relatively small proportion of the 6.9 million persons currently aided under the federal-state programs can be expected to be in the labor market.[8]

Today there is greater need than ever for preventive and rehabilitative services to counteract social as well as economic breakdown. There is need for education and training so that more people can become employable in an economy that provides jobs for the skilled and the educated. There is need for individualizing casework services in a period of history when divorce, out-of-wedlock pregnancy, juvenile delinquency, mental illness, and a host of other psychological and social problems are manifest for the economically deprived and for the financially adequate as well. It is this kind of public welfare program that is now being conceived in this country in the wake of the 1956 and 1962 Amendments.

In order to stay within the boundaries of our subject of staff development, we will not give in to the temptation of examining the various proposed solutions to the growing welfare coverage in this country. It would not illuminate our topic to discuss any of the recommendations to restrict the program, deny the need of the clientele, take them off relief, or expect that they pull themselves up by their own bootstraps. Deriving as they usually do from the self-reference of the proponents and not from objective knowledge, these recommendations are advanced as solutions to the problem, albeit not to the need which has created the problem.

Probably the most sensible and socially beneficial suggestions derive from those on the social welfare scene who have brought knowledge and experience to bear upon their ideas. They have observed that at least 64 countries in the world, and in fact all industrial countries except the United States, have some form of guaranteed income program as provision against the natural risks of urban, industrial life. Similar to our social security system, those programs, whether they are called family allowances, children's allowances, or medical insurance, are related to average economic need requiring no individualized budgeting, no assessment of a family's functioning, and, above all, no surveillance of the family's use of the money. Such institutionalized provision of economic security would, of course, remove a large number of people from the caseloads of public welfare agencies, would meet needs more humanely and successfully, and would reduce the requirement for skilled social work staff. As in those countries where such insurance programs exist, they could be administered by civil servants without social work skills, for the task of connecting the person with his allowance would be clerical and not evaluative or diagnostic.

The manpower required to carry out such a mass program would be large indeed, but the tasks required would be predetermined by eligibility factors built into the program itself. This process could be carried out by clerical and computer services and courteous, explanatory procedures. Training for this social and economic service, restricted to the tasks involved—to meet the public nicely, to evaluate eligibility appropriately, and to be accountable to the program auspices—requires intelligence and humane attitudes, not, as we have indicated, diagnostic skills, or the knowledge and judgment necessary to help clients with alternatives.

Training undoubtedly is essential for the staff of OASI, for example, but such training is of a very different character from that required by staff of public assistance and child welfare agencies in public welfare. The recent book published by the Social Security Administration, *Interviewing in Social Security,*[9] is an excellent illustration of an appropriate training instrument for staff in a social insurance program. It is entirely directed to the attitudes of staff and contains little technical information about the job of claims investigator itself. But the job is carefully defined and the investigator's activities are limited to carrying out carefully articulated procedures. Training is thus related to helping the worker to do his job as kindly as possible with his claimants.

The clarity of the claims investigator's job is not the only strength in the staff program of OASI compared with staff conditions in public welfare. Almost equally important is the factor of climate. One may visit any office of the OASI program and find good office furniture, pleasant space, excellent clerical and computer facilities, and a generally well equipped interviewing staff. This climate might be explained partially by the fact that as an insurance program it is financed by the claimant's previous contributions and made available automatically at the age of 65. One's eligibility for his grant does not depend upon his need for the money, or on his ability to stay within a budget. Moreover, the insurance program, based as it is upon a lifetime of economic independence through working and contributing, differs crucially from public welfare, which is usually the direct result of economic dependence and social inadequacy. These features differentiate the programs as far as public attitudes and support are concerned, and undoubtedly have an effect upon the quality of staff services.

Finally, the fact that OASI is a federally sponsored program has more than a little to do with its difference from state, county, or locally sponsored public welfare programs. According to Wilensky and Lebeaux, ". . . the closer one gets to the local level of government the less one finds welfare consciousness, and the lower grow welfare standards." [10] Conversely, the further away from local auspices, as in the OASI program, the less culpable the program in the eyes of the community, and the better the working conditions and services. When a program is compensated with social acceptance, good working conditions, defensible policies, and a clear focus, the key to successful staff practice is recruitment and selection of staff, sound administration, good personnel practices, and adequate salaries. Training of staff becomes a matter of induction into the job and continuing instruction as the job may change. In a large sense, the staff's development is a reflection of the surrounding climate; if that is conducive to sound practice, then half the job is done.

However, in this country in the mid-sixties we can see no indication of the readiness of lawmakers or taxpayers to embark on a mass social insurance program in which economic risks would be provided for. Moreover, again it must be brought to mind that a fairly large proportion of

the clientele known to public welfare agencies require social services that go beyond income maintenance. Those
families who are unable to keep up with the tight job
market may also be the ones whose housing is poor, whose
children are dissatisfied with school and fail or drop out
before they complete high school, whose opportunities for
recreation and cultural achievement are limited, whose
social relationships are affected by their incapacities, and
whose family life ultimately is jarred and threatened.
Those people will need the social services of public welfare agencies no matter how extensive social insurance
programs become in this country.

An interesting statement of the causes of dependency in
this country was made at the 1964 Roundtable Discussions of the APWA. It was mentioned that those who remain out of work for six months or more are most likely to
suffer permanent loss of jobs.

In the past ten years this group has increased from 6 to 16%
of all those who are unemployed. . . . While there are job
opportunities in service rather than blue collar work, non-pro-
duction rather than production jobs [limited educational at-
tainment prohibits employment in these jobs]. . . . Each year
250,000 children fail to complete elementary school; only 43%
of all adults have completed high school; over 23 million adult
Americans have less than 8 years of schooling and most of these
are functionally illiterate.[11]

It is not without significance that 20 percent of this latter
group are nonwhite, and that class as well as racial factors
play a role in the lowered level of education for such a
large proportion of this group of Americans. No amount
of simplified, unilateral job-training or rehabilitative approaches is going to make up for the slum living condi-

tions of 30 million people in this country. With these social and economic facts of deprivation existing in a period of high economic productivity and prosperity, it is evident that as long as poverty, discrimination, and lack of institutional programs are tolerated, public welfare services are going to be needed to counteract these deficiencies in American life.

In recognition of the inevitable continuation of this situation, there are countless revisions in the current system that can be made within the existing laws and practices. Such revisions may appear to be too shortsighted to some, but at least they are possible to achieve now, and for the present their acceptance would help clients and would relieve the heavy administrative burden in our public welfare agencies.

A primary problem in public welfare that needs to be dealt with on a policy level is that of excessive accountability within a public welfare program to higher levels of administration. This is not to say that clients would not have to achieve some degree of eligibility for a service, or that a social worker in public welfare would operate independently of legal restrictions or agency procedures. But the attention to detail has too often become the end rather than the means of helping. Human need, whether it be for food and clothing or satisfactory family relationships, may be categorized and counted, but there is a point where paper work and accuracy in accounting may take over the essential purposes of the public welfare program.

The odd thing is that there is almost total agreement in the field of social welfare, including the federal level of administration, that the task of the social worker in public assistance must be simplified if the client is to receive service and the social worker's job is to be made manageable. Many solutions have been offered; for example, that certain minimum funds be defined and agreed upon with which families of certain sizes and composition could manage. Then budgeting on an individual basis could be eliminated. Beyond this, certain types of cases could be identified where an additional statutory or discretionary allowance would be indicated, and responsibility of relatives eliminated.[12] Further simplification could be achieved by grouping budgeted items and preadding totals toward an income-conditioned pension type of public assistance.[13]

The means test in its present form is itself a built-in contradiction of values. It has often been suggested that we attempt to use professional casework skills while at the same time we are expected to help applicants come to terms with inadequate grants and harsh policies.[14, 15] Through our deterrent philosophy we place an excessive burden upon the client to demonstrate his need when we might, as Burns suggests, assume an average need, as in pensions based upon past contributions and in the social insurances. Moreover, as has often been pointed out, if it is common to trust the taxpayer to fill out his annual income tax return and the veteran to apply for his benefits, why not then the applicant for public assistance? The necessity to budget individual needs requires staff with the skills to differentiate among commanding needs, whereas a standard of need with the provision for special individualized needs would considerably reduce the burden of work, and would at the same time provide a sense of dignity and integrity for the client.

With respect to the application of social casework

skills, Wilensky and Lebeaux have stated the case strongly as they see the nature of the public assistance program in relation to the present staff situation: "Three outcomes of job evaluation are possible: provision of expanded professional services to supplement a streamlined eligibility determination operation; maintenance of only the limited amount of casework, . . . or complete elimination of the casework aspect of public assistance." [16]

The Organizational System and Administrative Controls

As staff practice is closely related to the attitudes of the community and the programs of public welfare in which practice rests, so is it also intertwined with the administrative controls that are exercised in the carrying out of programs. Those controls vary in accordance with factors that can be rationally assessed, or that at times may be arbitrary. Control is, of course, a necessary component of bureaucratic organizations. In describing the inevitability of an explicit structure of authority, Vinter states that "all organizations create means for ensuring that cooperative action is oriented toward desired objectives." [17] Those means may be used in an authoritarian way, as in the case of a punitive or threatened administrator—but it is rather as a rational process, a necessary component of all organizational structure, that control will be considered here as it interacts with staff practice. Controls over staff practice may be of an overseeing nature, such as when supervision as an extension of direct administrative regulations exacts proper action from the staff. Naturally, where the staff is untrained for its work, or where the job itself is not properly defined and organized, supervisory control becomes an extremely significant part of the administrative program. In the case of a professionally trained staff person —a social worker in public welfare—controls over practice are, theoretically, built-in through the staff member's experience in professional education and induction into the professional codes of practice. Thus, direct supervision as an instrument of control is not necessary to the same degree for this kind of staff. Of course, even the most highly skilled practitioner must be held accountable for his practice, and in public welfare agencies, as in private agencies, much of this accountability is determined through paper controls. From these the administrator may discover the extent of the worker's caseload coverage, his daily activities, the quantity of his production, and in some ways even the quality of his practice. These paper controls exist to a smaller or larger extent in all bureaucratic agencies, probably in proportion to the confidence the administrator has in his staff and, not incidentally, in his superiors.

While staff development is not necessarily synonymous with trust in staff, nor with complete freedom of action, it cannot take place in a social agency unless there is also a climate that is enabling and an atmosphere that induces staff to think and to make judgments without fear of recrimination. The administrator who asks his staff to account on paper or in person to him or his representatives for each action, no matter how detailed, or who insists upon absolutes in his expectations and does not accept the uncertainties that accompany learning, cannot hope to utilize a staff development program. The alliance of staff with rules that are ends in themselves can result only in mechanistic behavior, which, if supported by the administration, is a condition opposed to a staff's development.

As Merton has said, "[C]onformity to regulations can be dysfunctional both for realizing the objectives of the structure and for various groups in the society which the bureaucracy is intended to serve." [18]

Personnel Practices

The formal way in which staff is related to the administrative structure and its hiring, promotional, and dismissal policies, is through personnel practices. In the case of public welfare agencies, civil service is the primary organization providing those functions and exercising control over personnel policies. Civil service programs in this country, particularly on the federal level, can offer opportunities for flexible hiring of competent staff, maintain an open system of examinations and promotions, provide for release of inadequate personnel, and effectively serve the staff and thereby the organization. However, on local or municipal levels of government civil service does not always reach those heights of management.

Civil service, as the body in control of all levels of personnel within an agency as well as within all comparable governmental units, is usually faced with the task of managing professional, technical, administrative, clerical, and maintenance personnel within the public welfare agency, and also, in a municipality, within the fire, sanitation, health, hospital, police, library, museum, park, and recreational services. It is obvious that in this network of agencies there must be some equation of skills or tasks devised so that a central organization may budget for and administer such a huge personnel complex. Thus, professional social workers in different departments utilizing social work programs would have similar job and salary classifications. This is not so difficult to manage, as social work skills are transferable from one social agency to another. However, in communities where administrative or technical services are categorized under titles of management or supervision, the content of the job and the prerequisites for personnel will have different demands and cannot always be comparable. A casework supervisor in a public welfare agency will never be doing the same job as a lieutenant in the fire department, no matter how parallel their civil service ratings. It is characteristic of civil service that it must try to equate jobs while at the same time provide for different administrative, educational, and practice requirements within each agency.

How do civil service and personnel practices affect staff and its development? Actually, in innumerable ways, so much so that it might be said that without sound personnel practices carried out by a civil service program sensitized to the needs of a social agency and its staff, the development of this staff might well be impossible. According to a Brookings Institution study of professional personnel in New York City civil service, professional, technical, and managerial employees were "convinced that in all respects except job security and fringe benefits, employment outside of civil service would be more rewarding and would offer better opportunities for professional development." [19] It was also found that young professionals were not interested in civil service because of the red tape, politics, bureaucracy, and mediocrity they were convinced existed in municipal agencies of all kinds. This is a rather severe indictment of civil service, as was the 24.9 percent rate of turnover of social investigator staff in the New York City Department of Welfare in 1961.[20] To be sure, the content of a job, working conditions, salary levels, and work loads contribute to heavy turnover of staff and deterrence of qualified staff, but it cannot be overlooked that civil service practices themselves might also have a role in the unfortunate image of public service described in the Brookings study.

Consider only the New York City examination system for hiring and promotion. While this system may be unique to New York, variations of it may be found in many communities in this country. Under the system a person applying for a civil service position as a social investigator, whether or not he is professionally trained, must take an examination that is not always of the highest standard. Furthermore, when such an examination is given in a perfunctory manner and when fingerprinting, loyalty oaths, and a personal investigation are part of the hiring procedure, the tone of staff attitudes toward the agency is established at that point. A staff development program can be only of limited help in offsetting the impact of such a hiring experience.

As for promotional examinations, they too are in many cases geared to passing the largest number of personnel. Because of the agency's need for supervisors, for example, the examination can be so elementary as to denigrate the staff member as well as the job itself. The matter of determining fitness for a job through a written or oral examination is itself open to question. Often, a civil service department will permit no job evaluation to enter into its deliberations about promotion for a particular staff member, for fear that it will prejudice the decision against him. Examinations often do not reflect personality attributes or aptitudes for a job, but tend to protect the status quo. Ratings take into consideration veteran status and seniority as primary criteria, rather than qualities that reflect the level of staff service. Testing of memory rather than of reason and insight cannot qualify a staff for social work practice. It must be reiterated that a staff development program cannot in itself create a high quality of personnel; it can only work with the staff that is hired and promoted in the first instance. Without the total participation of civil service departments in the goals and values of staff development programs, the outcome of in-service training is inevitably limited.

A social worker who is a civil servant in a public welfare agency often feels contradictory identifications. A commitment to a career in a bureaucratic organization is not in all respects compatible with a commitment to a career as a social worker. For one thing, the two are not identical in their demand for knowledge and skills; the former is a commitment to a system, while the latter is to a service. The former rewards the worker for his loyalty to the organization, while the latter rewards him for the value of his services to the client. At any point these objectives may be conflicting. Moreover, in a city-wide or statewide civil service plan, the lack of differentiation between social work and non–social work personnel does not contribute to a proper classification of jobs in accordance with differentiated skills and other qualifications. The Brookings study [21] noted that among lower educational and occupational levels, personnel were concerned with job security, and in upper levels with challenge, creativity, and personal achievement. These latter attributes are the aspirations that a public welfare agency should ask of all of its social work staff, both professional and nonprofessional. The personnel system itself can promote them through respect for the value of the job to be done and for the worker, by demanding not the least but the most significance in performance.

In evaluating the control of civil service over public welfare practice and staff identification, it is helpful to view historically the differences that came about between the 1930s and the 1960s, much as we surveyed the change in the nature of public welfare programs over the last quarter of a century. In the 1930s, during a period of economic depression, personnel surged toward civil service because other work was almost impossible to obtain and there was always security inherent in a government job. Obviously, in the present period, when jobs requiring technical skills are in large supply, the necessity to identify with civil service has receded in favor of the preference for pursuing the professional model. Where a social worker does have a dual commitment, it is conceivable that his career or professional interest might conflict with his civil service image, as each status may well be in competition with the other.

As far as staff development is concerned, probably one of the most vulnerable aspects of civil service in public welfare is that it is so often a closed system. Those in the in-group, bound together through their civil service status, are frequently not professionally trained, and more often than not are resistant to outsiders, who are perceived as a threat to their vocational life. We find an extreme example of intrusion of civil service into social work practice when civil servants are not identified with social work but rather with the agency. Here we see the discouragement of outsiders, the denial of new ideas, and the continuing rigidity of entrenched procedures. There can be a primitive quality to the way a veteran staff will "gang up" to prevent interference with the system. Merton refers to this quality, in his discussion of sources of overconformity in a bureaucratic structure, as "devotion to regulations." [22] Administration-minded staff might adopt and encourage personnel practices devised by civil service, despite the fact that those practices might not always be sound or in tune with new trends—for example, promotion without professional qualifications, resistance to new professional lines parallel to their own, "bumping" qualified provisional staff as a privilege to be protected by the very staff who will not object to an unqualified person's conduct of his job. Dimock describes this phenomenon aptly when he says:

It is this kind of institutional behavior, sometimes manifesting itself in the form of resistance and obstructiveness and sometimes in the form of wholehearted response, which leads one to speak of the inner life of bureaucratic organization as being a force which is greater than the sum total of the obviously constituent elements. It is based upon long established meanings, nuances, ways of doing things; it is based upon an appreciation of what constitutes the long range interests of the career group.[23]

In this connection the Brookings study says: "The system automatically values experience gained on the inside more highly than on the outside," [24] despite the fact that experience gained outside the agency, particularly as a professional worker, might be more valuable. This closed system of promotion, favoring noncompetitive means, inevitably perpetuates inbreeding.

The Brookings study [25] points out that the merit systems must not necessarily require written tests, the rule of one, certification, or preferential use of promotion lists as opposed to open hiring. ("Rule of one" applies to the automatic selection of the next name on a promotional list to be given the next available job. A modification of this practice is the "rule of three," where a choice among three names can be made by a department head, enabling him to fit an individual to a job.) The United States Civil Service Commission recommends three basic objectives of a merit system, all of which provide for a flexible, open-minded hiring, promotional, and firing approach: competence, political neutrality, and equal opportunity. The study concludes, "With today's large, complex and technical government operations it is not possible to have a genuine merit system or to attain a high productivity without having highly competent executives in charge of programs and with discretion in choosing, placing and promoting employees." [26] In this connection, staff development programs as part of the administrative structure, concerned as they are with personnel, would function most effectively if they carried out a significant part of the personnel operation in public welfare agencies.

Working Conditions

To conceive of a staff development program without reference to the setting and physical atmosphere in which staff is to work is to use the "let 'em eat cake" philosophy.

Office space, availability of telephones, privacy for interviewing, and plentiful supportive services such as clerical
help, agency cars, file drawers that work, and efficient
maintenance, would probably do more for improvement
of the morale and production of a social work staff in public welfare than a series of training sessions. As long as the
professional staff that are increasingly drawn into public
welfare agencies are at the same time in great demand in
other public and private social agencies, office working
conditions are bound to become significant in the struggle
to attract and retain them. It is likely that the atmosphere
in which staff work each day vies with adequate salaries
as an important objective of personnel practices.

Staff morale is not an unimportant factor in the life of a
public welfare agency, nor is it unrelated to the staff development process. C. Wright Mills defined morale in two
ways, providing a rationale for the administrator in the
public welfare agency as well as for the staff itself. He
said:

Subjectively, morale would seem to mean a willingness to do
the work at hand, to do it with good cheer and even to enjoy
doing it. Objectively, morale would seem to mean that the
work gets done effectively, that the most work is done in
the least amount of time with the least trouble for the least
money. [27]

Mills suggests that we define the kind of morale we mean
when we talk about it. Surely, both kinds are crucial to
the effective operation of a public welfare agency and to
the personnel involved, and furthermore they are each
crucial to the other. Staff development programs owe
allegiance to both personnel and agency programs—in
fact, the recognition of their mutual interdependence is

the hallmark of an effective agency, a responsible staff, and a staff development program that is sensitively attuned to this mutuality.

Allocation of Tasks

The most important aspect of public welfare programs and administration as they affect staff development is the allocation of tasks. Unless the step is taken to clarify the tasks to be done most appropriately by professional, non-professional, administrative, and clerical staff, we might well ask what training is for. Our present lack of clarity has led to confusion and near chaos as public welfare programs have become increasingly complex and unmanageable for any single type of personnel. The Brookings study, in examining the question of use of higher skills, comments:

Manpower is wasted if it is used on tasks that should not be done, or should be done in a different way; if the people with the wrong skills are assigned to tasks, if the right people for the tasks are kept from them by artificial barriers; or if qualification requirements are not realistically related to duties.[28]

Thus, even if we could imagine a time when public welfare programs would employ completely professional staffs, it would still be essential to classify the responsibilities and functions allocated to them so as to remove the lesser tasks such as office duties that can be better assigned to clerks, routine work that can be done by mechanical devices, and technical jobs that can be more appropriately carried out by nonprofessional social workers. Differential allocation of tasks in accordance with occupational levels is a necessity in any impending hiring of professional staff. Without this step professionalization has no direction, and training will not be able to compensate for lack of clarity.

Merton explains this necessity in terms of effective bureaucratic functioning:

A formal, rationally organized social structure involves clearly defined patterns of activity in which, ideally, every series of actions is functionally related to the purposes of the organization. . . . The generality of the rules requires the constant use of categorization, whereby individual problems and cases are classified on the basis of designated criteria and are treated accordingly.[29]

Thus, the matter of classification and differential allocation of tasks is inextricably involved with the aims of the public welfare program, the practice of staff in carrying out those aims, and the development or training of staff.

Whenever one attempts to classify, the way of analyzing depends upon what one wants to achieve. The aim of classification in public welfare is, clearly, to make more efficient use of personnel with special and valuable skills, and to reassign tasks that are feasible for less qualified personnel. Whether the focus of allocation is to separate out levels of skills, to classify cases, or to find ways of spreading the influence of professional services through administrative devices such as practice teams or new service approaches like group treatment, the aim to be achieved is improved service in the face of an uneven balance between increasing demand and diminishing supply of professional staff. Allocation can thus clarify the goals of staff development, for only with allocation can it be stated with precision exactly what personnel are to be trained for.

There is no absolute guide to classification of workers, case problems, or tasks; much depends upon the knowledge, experience, and bias of the classifier. Attempts at classification and at putting schemes into operation have been reported from a variety of sources, all of which have tried to confront the situation of staff shortages realistically and have selected particular priorities in order to meet the personnel crisis.

Among the efforts made to differentiate staff functions and tasks, Richan [30] has made an excellent contribution in classifying worker roles and relating them to appropriate functions and client "vulnerability," or extent of need. Finestone [31] has pursued a similar line of inquiry in his differentiation of diagnostic from generalized functioning. In these approaches, Richan and Finestone have developed role distinctions from the standpoint of what the nonprofessional and the professional worker is each equipped to do in service to clients. This seems to be an extremely salutary approach for further study and testing. Epstein,[32] in her search to find a more effective plan for utilization of social work staff, has emphasized categories of cases, differentiating them according to problems to be worked on and services to be offered. Heyman [33] has approached the classification problem through a development of criteria whereby some cases would require professional casework skills and others would have a lesser demand.

A very different line of inquiry has been described in a National Institute of Mental Health pilot study [34] in which an experiment tested the hypothesis that carefully selected, mature people can be trained to do psychotherapy under limited conditions. While this study did not relate to classification problems, it demonstrated a selective procedure for utilizing available nonprofessional staff by delimiting their skills and aims in treatment. An illustration of another, somewhat similar approach to better utilization of untrained staff was described by Weed and Denham,[35] who attempted to train case aides perceived as potential professional social workers to do prescribed tasks with less complicated cases. The inference drawn from their experience is that proper selection of personnel and of appropriate cases would, with training, make adequate practice feasible. This approach is somewhat characteristic of many efforts to adapt the nonprofessional social worker to a preprofessional mold without classification of cases or tasks.

The effectiveness of one or another scheme of utilization of staff through classification by worker skills and tasks or by case problems depends always upon the premise of the expectations held. There are conceptual difficulties in all approaches, but the continued search for a theoretical model is essential in order to achieve some degree of accommodation between the imbalance of professional staff shortages and expanding definitions of public welfare services.

In considering the attempts that have been made to differentiate social work positions by assigning certain kinds of cases to professional and others to technical personnel, the key question is, "What constitutes a *kind* of case?" Immediately certain categories, some of them dichotomous, present themselves.

A common differentiation is often made between *simple and complex cases*. This kind of categorization depends, in the first place, upon the predetermination of what is simple and what is complex. Is a single, elderly client a simple case and a family with ten children a complex case? Not necessarily, if the aged person is disturbed and unpredictable in his behavior and the parents in the family have evident strengths that can be tapped to serve their children and themselves. Secondly, the complexity or simplicity of the case often lies in the eyes of the beholder. A layman may perceive a case as simple when the defensive behavior of family members keeps hidden serious conflicts that actually affect their social functioning. On the other hand, a social worker may recognize the boundaries of his work with a psychotic client to be so narrow while the client is disturbed, that complex though the case may be the work to be done is limited and "simple." To a nonprofessional or technical social worker who is skilled in meeting expressed needs and observing external dysfunctioning, a case may be simple because the problems are apparent and accessible to help. On the other hand, a skilled, professionally trained worker recognizes that no case can be presumed to be simple, because even the most elementary helping tasks must be performed within a psychosocial diagnostic process which is, in itself, highly involved and presupposes a grasp of theory and conceptualization of practice.

The classification of cases in these terms of simplicity or complexity does not rest on firm criteria, and is in fact a shifting scheme, responsive to subjectively determined prerequisites, the availability of appropriate personnel, and the state of our knowledge. The terms of classification themselves are value-laden, and like all values are reflective of changing commitments and are dependent upon cultural or social structures. To use an analogy, the common cold is a simple case problem, but only after it is so diagnosed and affirmed by the doctor. Whether the illness turns out to be a cold or pneumonia, the doctor's diagnostic process is the same. It is only when the patient is discovered to indeed have only a cold, that his becomes a simple case. In the same way, it can never be assumed beforehand that a social work case is a simple one— although limitations in the worker, restrictions in the agency's services, or restraints in the community may demand that we look no further.

A second, seemingly oversimplified approach to the classification of types of cases is that which describes *external versus internal emphasis* in the case problem. This attempt to dichotomize client difficulties denies the core of the diagnostic process, the connecting thread of inner and outer forces that combine to affect behavior in every individual, and the relationship of personality factors and the ego's functioning to the opportunities and limitations of the reality situation. Efforts have been made to categorize the clients' need for services with an external or social emphasis, like economic need, employment, housing, or some adjustment of living problems, as opposed to their internal or psychological needs, such as personality problems or marital, parent-child, or other relationship difficulties.

The erroneous assumption here is that difficulties in management, perhaps because they reflect observable symptoms of dysfunctioning, are external and thus simple. The most typical example of the effort to identify case problems in this way is the proposal that nonprofessional staff work with public welfare clients who need money, and professional staff work with those who are maladjusted.[36] While in an individual case it may occur that a client's economic need is not intertwined with his total adjustment, it is well known that the chief characteristic of the public assistance caseload in the 1960s is its residual flavor, the fact that economic need and social, personality, and functioning disorders are interrelated and reflective of each other. Moreover, as long as public welfare programs continue to require the individualized means test as the primary determinant of eligibility, all aspects of the client's life will necessarily be involved through this procedure, and the effort to differentiate public assistance from psychosocial problems will be futile. As long as need for money is not differentiated from need for services by policy, there will have to be some professional diagnostic assessment to differentiate one from the other. This process again suggests that the simple case may indeed be quite complex.

An equally significant factor related to the allotment of tasks based upon classification of case problems is that the determination of the kind of problem presented by a case must be made at the beginning of the client's contact with the agency. His request must be evaluated and his problem diagnosed before the agency can assess the simplicity or complexity of the case, or the direction treatment or service will take. This process of evaluation and diagnosis requires the highest level of social work skill, and only after it is done can tasks be realistically allocated.

In addition to the differentiation of cases according to their degree of severity, there is another approach to the assignment of tasks that is based upon the varied *functions of an agency.* These functions might be thought out in accordance with the direction of needs in the community or knowledge boundaries, but more often than not they are organized expediently around the availability of skilled staff. Therefore, we often find units of professional staff in public assistance assigned to family counseling services or services to multiproblem families, and other nonprofessional staff assigned to giving financial assistance. In child welfare programs we might find professionally trained staff assigned to unmarried mother and adoption caseloads, and untrained staff to foster care cases. The decision to give weight to one or another "unit of service" may have to do with community values or immediate pressures. For example, if unmarried mothers and their babies or cases where children are involved are of particular concern, those units may be given particular priority over cases of the aged or disabled in the use of available skilled staff. In this instance, the priorities of worker assignments are determined by administrative structure rather than by case demands.

The unit of service approach to the allocation of tasks is undoubtedly the easiest kind of differentiation to make; it contains a certain administrative orderliness in that its clear delineation avoids competition among staff for assignment, and provides a tidy and reasonable basis for a request for special funds for professionally trained staff. Yet, the inevitable result is usually that where potentially the greatest quantity of need exists, as in the general, undifferentiated public assistance caseload, staff that are less than professional are assigned, and it may never be known how complex the public assistance clients' problems are as long as no qualified staff are present to evaluate them.

Another common approach to the deployment of professionally trained staff is a straight *administrative* one. In this scheme administrative and supervisory positions are reserved for professional staff, and practitioner positions for untrained staff. Obviously this has merit, for in a situation of uneven balance between supply and demand of professional staff the few who are professionally trained may be most appropriately used in key, decisive positions where they would exercise the broadest influence on the agency's program. However, even this method of utilization of professional staff may not always be feasible or profitable from the point of view of the agency or the worker. For example, a new graduate or an experienced social worker might wish to remain in direct practice with clients. As we are aware, in many instances some workers are better qualified for direct practice than for supervisory or administrative positions, and they should be enabled to remain in jobs where they are best suited. Thus, even where the rule of thumb that professionally trained staff should be placed in higher positions could be applied, this plan would not meet the total needs of staff, and the agency would still be faced with having to delineate the functions of the professionally trained from those of the nonprofessional worker. Also, this approach would not be fruitful in an agency where some aspects of the job involved did not require social work skills even in the supervisory position. In such instances, the graduate worker's skills would be wasted.

Although the classification schemes we have touched upon have certain drawbacks, there seems to be particular validity to the Richan and Finestone proposals to differentiate workers according to their available skills and knowledge. Such an approach does not assume any difference in the needs of clients for trained staff, or any hierarchy of client need. Elaborating on this scheme in public welfare, we might conceive of the professionally trained social worker as having major responsibility for the welfare of the client in those areas for which he is trained; that is, in psychosocial diagnosis and treatment planning. This may include conducting the intake interview, leading staffing sessions where the facts about a family are brought together and are formulated into a diagnosis, and perhaps undertaking complex aspects of treatment where clients do not seem well motivated or where their ego defenses are rigid or fragile. The professional social worker's function would be modified by the program emphases in the agency; for example, in child welfare he might do the initial assessment in an adoption study or foster home evaluation or protective service. The untrained worker, under supervision of the professional worker, could make school and other collateral visits, collect the necessary social-medical data, arrange for clinic appointments, and even accompany the client when necessary. After foster home or adoptive placement, this worker could make routine supervisory visits to foster parents or adoptive parents where it has been determined that there are no outstanding problems, or he may arrange for clothing grants, camp vacations, day care, etc., where those services are deemed important in the staffing or supervisory conferences. In public assistance, for example, once the need for new housing is established and the problem areas involved with moving are clear to the family, the untrained worker may well be the one to help the family find and settle into a new residence. Where financial assistance is to be given, the professional worker might assess the needs with the family as long as a means test is required, and might structure the kind and amount of the grant. The untrained worker would give the necessary services and attention to the family, provided they are of a fairly routine kind where unexpected problems do not arise. If, as the case unfolds, it shows evidence of greater complexity, the professional worker could reenter the situation. The professional worker would thus maintain total responsibility for the family for as long as the services of the agency were needed, through direct attention, diagnosis and evaluation, and supervision of the untrained worker.

In the light of such a suggested plan for division of services and differential allocation of tasks to professional and nonprofessional staff, the question might arise as to what would happen to the caseworker's relationship with the client were he to share the case with another worker. It is hard to conceive of any social work service that would not involve a relationship with the professional or nonprofessional worker, and unless a controlled, professional relationship with one person were the primary goal of treatment, it would not seem harmful to a family to have two or more relationships in concert with the services being offered. As the state of social work knowledge has improved and has become increasingly communicable, the field has, perhaps, arrived at a point where it is possible to assess those tasks that can be done adequately by less than professionally trained social workers under professional supervision.

In *Training for Social Work: Third International Survey,* published by the United Nations and written by Eileen Younghusband, the Lahore Seminar Report stated that:

. . . to use auxiliary [or agency-trained] workers in this way [to perform under direction of professionally trained workers] was not a concession to an emergency situation but rather a recognition of a permanent need based upon a clear distinction of function between the professional and the auxiliary.

The Report from the Athens Seminar stated further that "the situation could only be clarified by analyzing the job to be done and the degree of skill required to do it, and then employing workers with appropriate skills for the job." [37] In public welfare or, for that matter, private welfare, social work is confronted with a crucial decision to accept or deny the inevitability of the technicians' useful place in social welfare programs not as preprofessional or even as nonprofessional workers, but as technicians with their own career line, their own functions, and their own tasks to perform.

One of the ways of approaching this problem sensibly is to determine what the professionally educated social worker is actually trained to do. What it is necessary to save him for will then become clearer. Above all things he is trained to exercise judgment, to make decisions about case problems, to weigh and synthesize evidence, evaluate significance, determine need, estimate strength and potentials, diagnose psychosocial problems, and use his personal resources consciously in his relationships with clients. No amount of agency training can develop the theoretical knowledge and the controlled practice skills which are acquired only through a long process of studious integration of classroom work and field work practice.

What, then, is left for the agency trained workers? There remain those tasks that are not practicable for the professionally trained workers to do as long as there are not enough of such workers and they must be conserved for functions more appropriate to their level. The agency trained worker can be instructed and supervised to secure information, to record data, to observe and identify problems that are apparent to him and will serve as clues to the professional worker, and to assemble facts. Moreover, he can be trained to interview and to take treatment actions that are carefully defined in direction and aim. The professional worker may then devote his time to applying the knowledge and skills with which he is equipped by education, while his nonprofessional teammate may supplement his own practice thereby, using skills that may be developed within the agency.

In this view of a differential allocation of tasks we are not concerned with a hierarchical system of services or clientele; the professional school is not to be perceived as a means of educating personnel for work with clients needing social casework services, and the agency as a means of training staff for work with clients needing public assistance. Rather, both professionally trained and agency trained workers would perform casework or individualizing services, but with differently defined duties and aims. As far as staff morale is concerned, it is already becoming increasingly difficult to reconcile staffs in public welfare with two kinds of training as well as two kinds of clients, dividing them into haves and have-nots, the ins and the outs. The system of allocation we are proposing relies on the determination of differential competence, which can be arrived at through objective means. Regardless of the way in which tasks will ultimately be allocated, the expectation is that some form of organizational clarity will be developed so that staff development will have a sense of direction and purpose. Without this, in-service training will serve only to support the present confusion.

Location of Staff Development in the Agency Organization

Within the context of the system of public welfare described in this chapter, where is the staff development program to be conducted? When it is viewed as one of the administrative components that affect staff practice, much as do allocation of tasks, agency controls, and personnel procedures, it follows that it should be placed as an integral part of the continuous, ubiquitous administrative process. For staff must be trained to do their assigned tasks and carry out the services of the program, just as they must be managed and enabled to perform their administrative functions. Staff development as an aspect of administrative structure should begin with the worker's hiring and orientation to his job, and continue throughout his tenure at the agency. Its effects should be pervasive, and its influence felt at every level of staff.

Professional manpower shortage notwithstanding, training programs are a prerequisite in any organization that performs a service or manufactures a product. According to the dictionary definition, "To train is to treat so as to bring to the desired form; to instruct or discipline in or for some particular art, profession, occupation or practice; to exercise, practice or drill." [38] The time and place of training and the selection of methods rest on a clear conception of the aims of training; in public welfare the primary objective is to develop in all staff the kind of knowledge and skills that will enable them to carry out the service program. There are two separate and discrete ways of accomplishing this objective. One is outside the agency, where the aim is increased professional education in a complete course of social work for as many workers as possible. The other is within the agency structure, where the aim is in-service training for all of staff so that they can carry out their carefully allocated tasks. While schools of social work may be enlisted to supplement in-service training programs, it is important to distinguish between professional education and in-service training, as only in-service training is conducted within the agency structure, accountable to its administration and subject to the strains and limitations of its organizational structure.

It is important to make this difference clear, because the very location of in-service training within a bureaucratic public welfare agency modifies educational aims and values and imposes demands that would never be tolerated in an academic setting. More often than not, the very selection of content to be taught in an agency training program is conditioned by the expectations of the personnel involved. In addition, approaches to teaching must often observe existing staff affiliations and "traditional" staff groupings, rather than abide by such considerations as the sequence of the material presented or the homogeneity of the group. Returning to the concerns of this chapter, personnel practices, salaries, controls, physical setting, staff morale, work loads, and job clarity, are all naturally of primary significance to public welfare staff, and each factor is an integral aspect of the staff's development. In-service training is but one part of this development, and educational methods used in in-service training programs may actually be quite insignificant in their effect upon practice in the light of the competing demands upon staff.

In order that the services of a staff development program be used to advantage, it must be viewed always as an administrative thread, a social work process weaving through all components of the agency and staff practice. It is unquestionably apparent that we are not viewing staff development as a separate unit or procedural device, since it has to do with staff at each turn in its connection with programs, personnel policies, administrative controls, training, and work with clients. As a process, staff development permeates the total agency and does not, in our scheme, vie for power as another bureaucratic structural service. To place staff development mechanistically as a unit by itself is to fly in the face of a fluid developmental approach, to add building blocks rather than to strengthen the foundation. Staff development—program, activity, process—emerges from a changing, interacting set of relationships. In a changing society, from which public welfare takes its cues, it is never possible to fix a program and to paste upon it other programs, for one can never then keep up with the inevitable demand for movement.

Staff development is a process which provides for perceiving personnel relationships with regard to the whole, to the corporate and bureaucratic society. As a process it reflects values, changing ideas, and balancing concepts. Dimock says:

Bureaucracies may be defined as the composite institutional manifestations which tend toward inflexibility and depersonalization. . . . In a complex environment . . . institutions have become large, relationships impersonal, and organization and procedures meticulously worked out; bureaucracy is a natural consequence.[39]

A staff development process, existing as a parallel phenomenon in a bureaucratic structure, may serve as a palliative, a buffer for staff against this impersonalization and rigidity. But it can only be effective when it is yet perceived as part of the ongoing structure, democratically subject to, but not reduced by, the same strains.

Eileen Blackey has expressed this dependence of training programs for their success upon agency attitudes, as follows:

Educational goals in any agency training program are in large part determined by the framework in which they are developed and they are only as sound and progressive as agency philosophy and administration permit them to be.[40]

Chapter Three

Professionalism and Graduate Education

In many respects the personnel shortage in all fields of social work reflects the pattern seen in other service professions.

Manpower studies have endlessly played the "numbers game": America must increase the number of its professionals from x to y by the year z. . . . Ignoring the difference in intellectual rigor between professional and vocational training, we *facilely* [italics added] assumed that if only funds and facilities were made available the nation would call into being as many professionals as it needed.[1]

The service professions have participated in the developing cognizance and articulation of human need and have demonstrated their particular expertise in the alleviation of many problems, sufferings, and demands of people. Yet, at a time when communities make known their urgent demands for more medical, paramedical, educational, and social services, it is ironic that the professions are unable to provide the personnel to staff those services.

Social work as an "emerging" profession is at present too overburdened to supply personnel for social welfare programs in public and private agencies, to provide services to clients, to develop the necessary means of preventing social breakdown, or to meet the requirements of massive rehabilitation and retraining programs to prepare people for living in our increasingly complex world. The demand for social workers to expand their services and improve their skills continues to increase, while hardly a toehold has been achieved in excellence. The necessity to keep up with current pressures to produce more and more professionals has resulted in attempts to lower standards of professional education and practice, as a small, and proportionally ever smaller, nucleus of workers spreads itself thin over the rapidly developing programs that need to be staffed. "The closer the professional moves to the center of American life . . . the more functions he is called upon to perform." [2] This phenomenon is often interpreted as an achievement, a triumph over the poor image of the unlovely past, a sure indication of the recognition—at last—of the professional social worker on the American scene. So it might be, were the jobs well done, were responsibilities fully carried out, were client needs met, and were the promise of more and yet more professional social workers possible to keep.

In the face of the imbalance in personnel that we have described, social workers as professionals have to make some immediate and crucial decisions regarding their responsibility to public welfare. In view of their commitment to the meeting of client needs, and the existing staff shortage that imposes limitations upon the provision of social services, there seems to be but one immediate course of action for social workers to pursue. They can, with haste, devise ways to utilize nonprofessional staff, to train them for the vocation of technical social worker, and to remain involved in their supervision and direction. Public welfare agencies which require really large quantities of personnel are already populated almost entirely by this technical staff; would it not be more efficient for the profession to recognize this fact and participate knowingly in their training and functioning? The professional social worker who seeks a position where he is in the company of only fellow professionals, and at the same time does not allow for flexibility in the use of technical staff or for recognition of this staff, has turned his back upon his primary responsibility to the very clientele which his profession exists to serve.

Yet, as we review the statistics and note again the small proportion of graduate social workers moving into practice in public welfare agencies, when we observe that a major part of the energy of the National Association of Social Workers (NASW) goes into efforts to gain legal regulation or certification so as to achieve professionalization at all costs, when we note the Association's hesitancy to include public welfare personnel in its membership, and when we assess the continuing preoccupation within professional social work to sustain particular hierarchies in practice, it is evident that the field of social welfare remains harassed by the resistance of many social workers to modify their all-or-none professional stance. We are not advocating reduction of standards for education within the professional schools; far from it. Rather, we are asserting that these standards can be justified only when highly skilled and knowledgeable people exist along with an army of social work technicians who are trained and fit for the huge quantity of tasks confronting the total field of social welfare. As Carr-Saunders and Wilson commented over thirty years ago:

Social and industrial changes are rapid—the "laborer" is fast becoming a figure of the past. It may be that even if all men do not come to be trained in some elaborate technique, everyone will belong to a vocational association upon which will be devolved a responsibility for the good conduct of some aspect of social or industrial organization. In this manner there may be an extension of the professional attitudes downwards as well as outwards.[3]

Before we look at some of the role differentiations involved in this inevitable "downward" extension, let us examine further the interesting phenomenon of resistance to it.

In an article by William Goode entitled "Encroachment, Charlatanism and the Emerging Professions," there is a classic analysis of this resistance that will serve as a beginning for our discussion:

The emotion laden identification of men with their occupation, their dependence on it for much of the daily meaning of their lives, causes them to defend it vigorously and to advance its cause where possible. If a new occupation claims the right to solve a problem which was formerly solved by another, that claim is an accusation of incompetence, and the outraged counter-accusation is, of course, "encroachment." [4]

While a task force of social work technicians in no way resembles a new occupation, the effect of its existence may call forth the cry of "encroachment" much as if the threat were real. Goode develops his point further when he makes a "sociological guess that the most severe skirmishes" in the development of an emerging profession would occur between it and the occupational group closest to it in "substantive and clientele interest." [5] The experience of professional social work is probably unique in that members have traditionally practiced in many host agencies such as hospitals, clinics, courts, and schools, where in team relationships with other professionals social workers have enjoyed less than equal status. Social workers have in fact laughed at themselves in their sisterly or daughter-like relationship toward psychiatrists and other medical men, who are seen in big brother or father roles. Seldom, if ever, have professional social workers been in a position of superior status when working in concert with specialists. That is, never until now, when community pressure and public legislation have literally forced upon the social work profession an awareness that it has to do the public welfare job itself, or else enjoin a significant number of others to do it. Again, to quote Goode: "Professional monopoly of a scientific field seems impossible or absurd. . . . [There is] no precise definition of the juncture at which the client may properly call on professional help . . . rather, [there is] a definition of skills and knowledge, that is, of the field." [6] Surely, in the modern public welfare agencies—the near-giant bureaucracies with vast quantities of work to be done— tasks can be defined and allocated so that skilled and effective technicians can be fitted into the social work scheme without affecting at all the integrity of the profession. In any case, there are better guarantees of protection of the profession when it defines the tasks and exercises controls over the technical occupational group. Moreover, it may soon happen that professional social work will be without a choice in the matter; for it is the community and the community alone that will admit a profession, support it, and approach it for the services and skills it can provide. Without the community at large—the very community that is demanding action—the profession would soon waste away. Thus, in order to survive, professional social work must demonstrate that it will meet the community's demands in one way or another.

In the present period when the profession of social work is in the process of accommodating itself to the pressure of personnel demands, it is natural that the inequality of knowledge and skills between professionals and technicians would present a challenge to both groups. It is also understandable that professional social workers, who are in the process of carving out a place among American social institutions, would concertedly strive to achieve certification and legal regulation. In their drive they have succeeded in excluding nongraduate social workers from membership in the NASW. In this period of history when nongraduate workers in the social welfare field outnumber graduates by a ratio of more than four to one, ever increasing numbers of nongraduates remain outside the mainstream of social work despite their overwhelming presence in welfare programs. To say the least, this situation has not promoted good feeling between the two groups, and in addition has widened the gap between the two levels of practice. Public welfare staff across the country are generally unorganized, except as they may find identification in the APWA, which is a membership and not a professional organization. Increasing professionalization of social workers will further separate public welfare staff from affiliation with graduates, and unless efforts are made to find some link between the two groups it will become progressively difficult for professionals to practice in public welfare agencies. A further consequence of this demarcation between the two groups is that the nonprofessional staff might seek a more welcoming field of practice—such as public administration—with which to associate itself.

The problem of professional or scientific control of practice within a bureaucratic structure has been given much attention of late, implying as it does the question of the entrance of professional influence into bureaucratic organizations. We have mentioned that the professional social worker in public welfare suffers from conflicting identification with the organization and the profession, and it is not unusual that the person who remains within the bureaucratic organization finds his ties to the profession weakened under the pressure of everyday work life. The conflict, however, is not without possibilities of alleviation.

Bernard Barbar suggests ways of reducing the strains between professional roles and organizational necessities.[7] First, he recommends clearly differentiated role structures—the categorization of tasks that we have been discussing here—so that the functions carried on by professional social workers are different in kind, quality, and direction from the tasks that are practiced by the technical, nonprofessional worker. It is obvious that this distinction in role, and the mere fact that each type of personnel has its own definition of function clearly perceived by each, will lessen the strain and will give validity to both career efforts.

Second, Barbar recommends a differentiated authority, with professionals responsible to other professionals in the administrative hierarchy. Naturally, it is reassuring when the "boss understands because he has been there," has had his own indoctrination into the profession, and so can recognize the direction of the professional's practice. Such an accommodation to the inevitable pull between professional practice and bureaucratic organization presupposes that commissioners of welfare be experienced, professionally trained social workers, particularly since social work requires the support and outlines that can best be provided by its own membership.

The third recommendation that Barbar offers as a way to reduce strains is that rewards should be offered that are commensurate with the aims and practices of the professional involved in a bureaucratic organization. The opportunity to go to professional meetings, to write, to attend courses, to get salaries in line with NASW standards—all of these things enhance the job to be done and make for the legitimate kind of prestige that often accompanies professional standing. Again, we can recognize the multiple career lines we have mentioned before—the possibility of working in a bureaucratic agency like a public welfare department and performing a professional job in an atmosphere conducive to the highest levels of practice, different from the job done by a technical team member who has his own career line to pursue and his own job definition with commensurate rewards.

Turning now from the aims of the profession as they relate to community demands, we find yet another compelling reason for the professional social worker to promote the use of technicians as members of the social welfare team. This is a period in history when knowledge is developing rapidly and the professional social worker must be able to keep up with its advances and modify his practice accordingly. One of the hallmarks of a professional is alertness to change and readiness to adapt his practice to necessity. Thus, the professional must be freed from those tasks that have been tested and found suitable for another to carry out. Moreover, if the graduate professional is asked to take on tasks that are not challenging and do not demand the application of theory and skill that he has learned, he will inevitably change his job and move on to one that is more demanding; if, indeed, he does not move out of the profession entirely.

Even though the professions guard their accepted functions jealously, when a task has been carefully developed and routinized it may become apparent that the clientele may not require the services of a professional staff person. When new practices are developed and refined they can be taught to technical personnel who may not be accomplished in theoretical knowledge. Far from following a Gresham's Law, where bad practice drives out good, the release of some tasks may well provide additional time for the professional social worker to go about his true work —that of discovery, prevention, and treatment or rehabilitation.

One of the ways to arrive at a true differentiation of professional social work from technical practice is to examine the characteristics of professional education. This, after all, is the chief indicator that draws the line between the professional and the nonprofessional worker. Only as the differences are fully reckoned with will it be possible to address ourselves to in-service training as a discrete method in staff development in public welfare agencies.

Younghusband has commented upon the differences between professional and auxiliary workers as follows:

The essential distinction thus rests upon functions performed rather than upon whether or not there is supervision or whether or not the task is inferior . . . confusion and dissension only arise when different functions are not clearly distinguished and suitably qualified persons employed to fulfill the appropriate function.[8]

Thus, it would seem that professional education for one function would naturally differ from technical training for another.

Any attempt to equate academic with agency training programs would only diffuse our conception of both. The two differ in objectives, method, and content, even though they may share certain values.

Whitehead defines a profession as opposed to a craft as follows:

[A profession is] an avocation whose activities are subject to theoretical analysis, and are modified by theoretical conclusions derived from that analysis. . . . [A craft is] an avocation based upon customary activities and modified by the trial and error of individual practice.[9]

The education of a professional, then, as distinguished from the training of a craftsman or technician, is aimed at developing a base of theory upon which the individual may draw methodically in a self-contained, self-conscious way in his practice. Everett C. Hughes's discussion of professionalization [10] includes among its themes that of a balance of detachment and interest. In his view the professional pursues and systematizes pertinent knowledge, seeking an intellectual base for the problems handled.

"[Professional knowledge] takes those problems out of their particular setting and makes them part of some more universal order." Hughes also includes a balance between knowledge of the universal and the particular, and between intellectual and practical pursuits.

Other writers, such as Barbar, do not recognize quite the same distinctions between the professional and the technician, seeing the differences rather in degree and in the context of the attributes common to all occupational behavior. Among the attributes Barbar recognizes as characterizing professional behavior are:

1. Generalized and systematic knowledge.
2. Primary orientation to the community interest rather than to individual self-interest.
3. A high degree of self-control of behavior through codes of ethics internalized in the process of work socialization and through voluntary association.
4. A system of rewards (monetary and honorary)—a set of symbols of work achievements as ends in themselves.[11]

Goode defined professional education as "a prolonged specialized training in a body of abstract knowledge, and a collectivity or service orientation."[12] Naturally, social work began as other professions, by codifying its trial and error experiences and ultimately translating them into theory to be tested and applied and then to be communicated to students of the field. Talcott Parsons encapsulated this in his statement that "what is best to do rests now on theory rather than on how the fathers did it."[13] In place of the pragmatic or doctrinaire approach, the professional's authority rests in his competence, his grasp of knowledge, and his skillfulness.

As the profession of social work moved beyond the

place where training was of an apprenticeship sort and personnel were taught setting by setting, beyond the time when rule of thumb practice prevailed and was unintegrated into theory, and beyond the status of volunteerism and lay leadership, the locus of training moved gradually from agency to technical school or institute of training, in response to specific community needs or to the initiative of a person or group of persons who believed that training for social work service was important. From this experience of collecting knowledge, it was natural that generalization and universalization of this knowledge would follow. Today, in the United States at least, professional education for social workers occurs mainly within an academic setting, as the university is the logical locus for the learning and teaching of what has become a theory of social work practice. It might even be said that the more firmly established the profession became in the eyes of both the community and the university, the more highly developed were its theoretical underpinnings and the greater its distance from the settings in which practice is carried out. This notion provides one of the most significant rationales for agency or settings-based training programs.

Many professions maintain the vital connection between theory and practice by having practitioners become teachers, and by the provision of student practice or field work experience during the academic training period. But the aegis of professional education is nevertheless the university.

It is the business of the university to educate, to provide for the development and teaching of theory, to inform and instruct. The university's primary concern with practice of any sort is as a testing ground for theory; it does not exist to give service, or to get the actual job done. Obviously, the university cannot be the only source of instruction; training for specific jobs can in fact be done best within specific settings. It is this kind of training that we are exploring in this book, and it is essential to understand how it differs fundamentally from university-based training.

It is important to examine some of the limitations of professional education in terms of its ability to provide the requisite social welfare personnel. Our interest is not to give a critique of professional education, but rather to show that it has proved impossible for universities to educate a sufficient number of professionals to man the field.

In order to qualify for graduate study, a college student must have earned good grades and demonstrated his intellectual capacity, and he must fulfill whatever qualifications his particular graduate school considers important. Also, professional education is costly in time and money. Attending a professional school is an act of postponement, requiring two years of preparation before the individual can earn money, fame, or any other reward. We must consider these demands in a society where achievement and immediate concrete results are important, and where a graduate student, after study, is prepared only to enter his chosen profession. Moreover, the cost of professional education is generally beyond the means of most potential students, even if they have demonstrated ability and interest. The time, cost, and capacity to postpone one's goals and to remain in school beyond the age of normal wage earning requires an uncommon degree of motivation, ability, and resourcefulness. The selection and recruitment of such students is difficult enough for any one profession, but when we consider that all professions and many skilled crafts are competing for competent personnel, we see that the problem of providing for personnel in the social work field is seriously compounded.

Furthermore, the facilities of graduate schools are limited because of lack of funds and lack of qualified teachers. In their concentration on educating practitioners, the emerging professions like social work have not had time to develop teachers of their own students. In addition, professional schools need experienced and qualified practitioners as teachers, and those people are ordinarily on the highest salary or income level of the profession. Consequently, there is built-in competition between the practice and academic circles for the few expert people at the top of the personnel pyramid. Perhaps time will take care of this in the emerging professions as it has to some extent in the established ones, but in this decade the lack of qualified personnel has affected the graduate school of social work just as it has the field of practice.

Returning now to the characteristics of professional education that differentiate it from in-service training, we may ask who determines what is to be taught in the graduate school. What is the primary reference group to which the graduate school is affiliated? Without any doubt it is the profession itself, even though, as any social work educator will confirm, the pull toward identification with the parent university may be as strong as that toward the profession.

William Goode, in another of his scholarly statements on the professions, refers to the community-like attributes of a profession, whose association and members control admission to training and "require far more from its trainees than the continuing community demands." [14] There are, of course, degrees of professional influence upon inductees during their graduate training. Apparently, the older, more established professions can afford to be more demanding than the emerging professions in the time required for professionalization. As Goode mentions:

Some professions like the clergy, the military and medicine almost isolate their recruits from important lay contacts for several years, furnish new ego ideals and reference groups, and socialize their behavior in the shadow of the professional.[15]

In social work education, this pattern is followed for two years, where the student must have full-time residence, cannot carry a job while he is at school, ordinarily must attend classes for most of two days a week and field work for three, and must in addition read and prepare assignments. At one count his total commitment came to 51 hours a week. In effect, this schedule requires almost complete isolation of the student from other activities and interests, often even from his family.

Not only is the student's time dominated almost completely by his school requirements. His induction into the profession takes place through articulated and subtle means, in the classroom and in his field work agency, where by concept and precept his teachers and field instructors lead him toward the "right" way, and short of indoctrination help him to achieve as complete an identification as possible with the aims, values, and ideals of social work. This is accomplished as the professional teacher and those around the student in his field work agency serve as models of thought and behavior; through imitation at first, the student comes to recognize the conduct that is approved and rewarded. In the process of exposure to history and tradition he is introduced to the great names of the past, the founding social work institutions, the good and the bad, the comical and the serious that have gone before. By these methods the student in a graduate school of social work is given opportunities for identification with people and causes. Not the least of ways in which identification is strengthened is through enunciation of the future aims of the profession—the unknowns that the student will be expected to make known and the grand causes yet to be tackled, causes with which the student himself will be called upon to cope.

The graduate school of social work, then, uses means over and above direct teaching of content and skills to bring about professionalization. All those means are important, even though an irascible student may, at times, complain of "brainwashing." They are important not because they constitute the established way, but because the student must rely on them until he becomes experienced enough to adapt or change them for the next generation of students.

Important as professionalization through indoctrination and presentation of behavior models are to the graduate student's development of attitudes, the fact remains that the chief value of professional education lies in the acquisition of knowledge and the utilization of skills relevant to the carrying out of social work practice. To a very large degree, the core of this practice is an intellectual one; thinking and disciplined verbalization are the tools of the professional social worker. As this fact has become increasingly recognized, reliance upon university rather than agency training has become more marked in social work training. Brownell summed up this evolvement of professional education in his statement that:

The influence of universities is clearly evident in the development of professional curriculums. No longer are they dominated by a narrow vocational outlook emphasizing methodology and techniques of practice . . . but the programs rest on the sciences as a foundation.[16]

In the modern profession of social work, the foundation of social science is not completely in evidence, partly because of the present limitations in social science theory, and partly because this heretofore "borrowing" profession is still in the process of developing an identifiable social work theory, which will undoubtedly achieve greater scientific validity as social work research itself develops its method and content. Yet there is every indication that social work education, based upon theory and where possible upon science, has moved well beyond the pragmatic stage of evolution.

The goals of professional education can, in fact, be enumerated. The graduate will be a competent practitioner first, then perhaps a creative leader. As a professional he will direct his efforts toward the service of others, using his personality discriminately, subduing his personal needs, and accommodating himself to the needs and requirements of his clientele, the individuals, families, groups, or community which he serves. He will regard new knowledge highly and continue to read, study, and evaluate materials that may be drawn from his colleagues' experiences or disciplined research efforts.

Ruth Smalley, in discussing the necessity for a professional school, has most literately assessed social work education as needing to include:

. . . the continuous selection and ordering of a body of knowledge to be transmitted, the development of educational experiences, and the sustaining of an educational process most conducive to the student's becoming able to use his knowledge and himself in a professional activity for which he is responsible to his profession and to society. It asks of the student a degree of self-investment, self-awareness, self-development and self-discipline which alone can make learned knowledge useful toward the achievement of any profession's purposes.[17]

The crucial matter of competence should be the distinguishing feature of the professional social worker. In any assaying of his competence upon his graduation from a school of social work, should emphasis be placed on his knowledge, or on his skill? These two components are so closely interrelated that it is impossible to clearly separate them. As the practitioner performs his particular functions with intelligence and craftsmanship his actions are always based, consciously or unconsciously, upon his knowledge. That the graduate school of social work teaches skills at all is a credit to its ingenuity and organization of time and effort. Teaching of knowledge is usually reserved for the university, while skills may be learned in the field of practice. Probably the single feature that once characterized apprenticeship training was the teaching of skills rather than knowledge, and skills are quickly outdated unless they are so ordered as to be related closely to developing theory.

In the combination of art and science that prevails in social work practice, the professional student acquires a basis of theory that includes a range of scientific reliability. He achieves competence only as he is able to utilize this knowledge, select from it, integrate its parts, come to terms with its inevitable contradictions, and complete the process by applying it appropriately in his actual, living experience with his clientele. McGlothlin, in his *Patterns of Professional Education,* summarizes this process of application as "The process by which the practitioner draws upon knowledge and skill, filters them through the screen of his personality, and applies them in a situation calling for the services of the profession." [18] The test of professionalism, therefore, is competence, and the test of competence is application.

When a professional social worker and a social work technician both work at their appropriate tasks, although those tasks may look similar from a superficial point of view—that is, they may involve investigating the same kind of social situation—the application of knowledge of theory and method is what differentiates the two workers. Both may be warm, related, personable, and intelligent, but one has been given a knowledge base and the other has learned his tasks through trial and error or through specific example in training. The influence of in-service training upon the social work technician might reduce the margin of error, but it will not provide a body of knowledge or a development of skills comparable to those of a professional social worker.

In what way does the graduate student acquire knowledge and skills? What are the methods and content that characterize professional education in social work? In the same way that one can establish a relationship between art and science, and between the knowledge and skill or theory and practice base of social work, so a decided connection can be noted between content and method. The way in which the method of social work is taught is colored by the nature of the content.

In theoretical content, first of all, there is the organization of basic concepts and principles about social welfare and social work practice. Then there is the subject matter related to social welfare itself—its history, programs, limitations, and practice boundaries. There are the related sciences of sociology, psychiatry, medicine, and psychology to be integrated into the student's total knowledge base, and there is research method to be learned. Finally, there is a social work method to be taught, developed by theoretical means from the total contribution of knowledge in the curriculum. Throughout, the student must assume a philosophical stance in each aspect of his practice and in his role as a social worker in the modern world.

The practice content derives primarily from his field work, where the knowledge gained in the classroom is selectively applied, under careful instruction, to an array of actual situations which are themselves chosen in accordance with the level and pace of the student's learning needs. This application of theory is significantly different from the agency training experiences of the nonprofessional worker, because the latter has a different kind of responsibility. A staff member has a commitment to his job, and the aim of his training is to improve his specific practice, not to achieve a thoroughly informed understanding of what he is doing, or of why and how some methods work and others do not. Field instruction in graduate school is educational in nature as regards the selection of tasks to be done by the student, the intensity of his instruction, his self-involvement in the process, and the expectations of his practice. An educational point of view, for example, would mean that the field instructor would evaluate progress in the student's practice as an indicator of his learning. A training supervisor in an agency setting must demand not only progress but some standard of achievement that is acceptable to the agency. This is not to say that the social work student has no standard to reach; on the contrary, his standard is high, but the process of his achieving it is more significant, for part of the practice knowledge he must have is awareness of the steps he takes toward his learning objectives.

In summary, field work for the graduate social work student is a creative, challenging experience with the chief objective of giving the student a controlled arena in which to put his knowledge of theory to work; not to get the job done, although this might be serendipitous. Quite the reverse is true in the case of agency training, where the job must be done and any learning that may come of it secondarily is a "bonus" to the worker and the agency.

Another significant aspect of professional education that differentiates it from agency training is the fact that it is generic in its focus; that is, it aims to educate the student across the lines of all fields of social work, certainly beyond the confines of particular agency practice, and even across the boundaries of particular methods. Thus, for example, the program and policies of a public welfare agency may be outside the learning experience of a professional student while he is in school, yet, as with other agencies in which he does field work, the content of the agency's practice must be perceived by the student in the light of the aims of the school curriculum.

It has often been said that the school trains for the field and the agency for its own practice. In the light of this generic trend, agency training has become essential for the graduate social worker just as for the technician, because each requires induction into the practices of the agency in which he will work. The mobility of social workers is renowned, and as they move from agency to agency they continue indefinitely to need agency training. Therefore, we have come to view their in-service training as fulfilling a different but supplementary role to their graduate social work education.

Keeping in mind the broad factors that differentiate professionally educated social workers from agency trained technicians, let us examine the role of professional schools in agency training programs. Earlier, we commented on the increasing pressure by the community, the profession itself, and the social agencies—particularly public welfare agencies—upon the schools of social work to participate more actively in the training programs of the agencies. We shall have more to say about this question later when we talk about in-service training, but here we shall concern ourselves with the problem from the point of view of the professional school.

We have pointed out previously the impracticality of projecting a goal of total professional education for all public welfare personnel, because of inherent limitations to be expected in the personnel as well as in the schools. Here we are considering the use of schools by groups of personnel under the sponsorship of their agencies, not by individual applicants for graduate education.

There is no question at all that the schools could provide the facilities for teaching, the faculties, the libraries, the curricula, and even the time during the academic year, in summers and in evenings, to fill agency training needs. It is also evident that public welfare agencies have masses of untrained staff and almost limitless funds to pay for courses, or for teachers and the full services of the schools; even the workers' time could be made available if the agency administrations were convinced of the validity of sending employees to classes while on their jobs, with compensatory time off. It is therefore unthinkable to some that the availability of educational facilities and the complementary availability of personnel and finances cannot provide the answer to all training problems once and for all.

There are at least four reasons why such a mass training type of program would not be effective. In the first place, if it were to be viewed as in-service training, then the school faculties involved would be quite out of their element, as they would not be knowledgeable about the agency's practices. Moreover, it has happened that when groups of public welfare staff have been exposed to courses with professional content not related then or later to their own practice, either they have become dissatisfied with the way things were done in their agency and have resigned or have been discouraged with the disconnectedness of school and agency programs. This is not a happy objective. As we shall see in our discussion of in-service training, class work taken by a nonprofessional person in a school of social work while he is employed in an agency is not directly or even indirectly helpful unless the class experience is somehow integrated, consciously and deliberately, into the agency's program of in-service training. It is not important here to wonder whether that integration would take place by means of the faculty person attending agency programs, the agency training person attending the school classes, or parallel group sessions taking place in the agency before or after the school sessions. However this were to be done, it would have to be coordinated somehow, just as the teaching of knowledge and skills is coordinated on another level for the graduate student. Even so, efforts at integration would not prove entirely satisfactory for school or agency, because so often the aims of education are not identical with the aims of an agency program.

A second reason why a mass education program for public welfare personnel sponsored by the agency would have severe limitations lies in the reaction of the staff. A common phenomenon of resistance to learning occurs when staff "volunteer" for class sessions, but when attendance is not truly voluntary because it is tied up with job evaluation, salary increases, and the like. Naturally, the resistance to learning in an involuntary class would be even more in evidence. In these situations workers have been observed to challenge the teacher to tell them something they did not know, to fall asleep during the session, to heckle, and literally to undermine the intended purpose of the class. Unless these groups were completely voluntary, it is doubtful that mere attendance would promote learning, much less affect the worker's practice upon his return to the agency.

A third reason also has to do with staff, but more in their resistance to professional education and their adherence to their own ways of practice than in outright resistance to learning. In some ways this response is the most dangerous, in that new content and method being taught in the school will be taken lightly or will be intellectualized and serve to close off for the worker recognition that he is not completely trained and that there is more to learn, particularly in the disciplined use of himself with his new knowledge. Self-discipline is probably one of the most important skills to be learned and it is generally acquired only through full-time attendance in graduate school, where opportunity is provided for integrating classroom courses with carefully supervised field work. This opportunity is ordinarily not available in an agency setting, where staff is primarily working and not necessarily learning. Thus, the lack of integration of content and practice constitutes a serious hazard if we attempt to make the agency or an extension program in a school a substitute for the graduate school in formal teaching of theory without the opportunities to learn corresponding practice skills.

Finally, there is a decided threat in such programs for the schools and for the standards of professional education. For if one lends one's services to an educational program that demands less qualitatively than is expected of full-time students, and such a program is viewed as good enough for public welfare, then perhaps, one may reason, it should be good enough for graduate students at large. The fact of the matter is it is not good enough for either group. By promoting pseudoeducation, graduate schools of social work would be participating in downgrading the function of the largest and most crucial body of staff in social welfare, as well as endangering the integrity of their own educational programs.

In view of these cautions about using schools of social

work in lieu of in-service training programs, how can the facilities of graduate schools best be utilized in the service of training social workers in public welfare? Beginning with the agency's own in-service training program and its relationship with the schools, there is a range of possible programs that can be considered, programs that have a greater degree of feasibility because they are clearly either in-service training or an extension of it, or full professional education or that sector thereof that might be undertaken part time.

One such program, the extension course, requires precise definition so as to eliminate confusion between in-service training and professional education, and to avoid the pitfalls involved in undertaking mass extension courses without regard to selection of students or integration of content. Extension courses given in a school of social work should derive from the practice and training needs of the agency, and should be geared to the functions of the staff and the agency. They are not identical with courses given by the school in its curriculum for graduate work, since they are not to be construed as courses in professional education, but rather as extensions of the agency's in-service training program. In fact, such courses become necessary when the agency needs the skilled help of professional teachers to enrich and enlarge the in-service training program.

The courses would offer no academic credit, and while they may be given either at the school or at the agency, they are usually more constructively offered on the school's premises if this arrangement is at all possible. The students then are free from the distractions and irritations of the office setting, they are close to library facilities, and most important of all, in the atmosphere of an academic institution they are exposed to the serious approach of professional education. However, if professional teachers are available within the agency, and if the setting provides quiet space and reading facilities, the extension course does not necessarily have to be given at a school.

From the school's point of view this definition of agency extension courses helps to avoid the hazard of lowering standards of graduate education, since such courses carry no entrance requirements and bear no relationship to the ongoing curriculum. The introduction of an extension course belongs within the province of the agency, which decides when it shall be taught, who shall attend, and the general subject matter desired. It is, of course, usually paid for by public welfare funds and derives from the training demands of the agency. The actual planning of the course must be a joint process between the agency and the school, but the final decision as to course content, teaching method, and conduct of the course itself must remain with the school and ultimately with the teacher in the classroom. It would indeed be unfortunate if extension courses became substitutes in any sense either for professional education or for continuous, agency-based in-service training. Each of these has specific, necessary goals and methods which cannot be met by any number of extension courses. An extension course program can only help to enrich in-service training.

A second form of program that can be made available to staff of a public welfare agency is one that remains completely under the direction of the school of social work, even though the agency may play a significant role in encouraging its staff to take part in it. This is generally known as a part-time course program, usually provided at the school in the evenings during the academic year. These courses are, in a sense, an extension of the school's own program of professional education, and schools vary in limiting the amount of credit a student is permitted to carry on a part-time basis. As opposed to the extension course, the selection of students, subjects, and time and sequence of courses, is determined entirely by the school, and agency personnel must accommodate themselves to the school program.

If an agency wishes to encourage staff to attend elementary courses, on a beginning master's degree level, then it may contribute toward the cost of the students' attendance. In many communities, schools of social work provide part-time tuition fellowships, often in accordance with the number of graduate student field work placements available to them through the agency. The value of this kind of program is that it may serve as an introduction to professional education for competent but wary personnel, and it may screen out those who are not up to the level of instruction and would not profit from full professional education. As the content is related to professional education and not directly to the program of the agency, part-time social work courses cannot be expected to immediately affect the daily practice of the staff members, although of course some may see connections, independently or with the help of willing supervisors.

A third type of program applicable to the relationship between professional education and public welfare practice is that of staff participation in full graduate training —full-time, two year attendance at a school of social work while on educational leave with or without pay. The number of fellowships paid for by the government for public welfare staff to attend school is steadily increasing, as are the less beneficial work-study arrangements. This type of program offers only a partial solution, for it is doubtful, for the reasons mentioned earlier, that full-time graduate study would be possible for the masses of staff even if they were to apply and qualify. In any case, the number of graduates would not be sufficient to make a significant nationwide addition to the professional staff potentially available to public welfare agencies.

To the extent that personnel are encouraged to attend school on a full-time basis, the agency has a role in the selection of applicants for its educational leave, scholarship, or work-study programs. Actually, this process usually takes an inordinate amount of administrative and staff development time in an agency, even though the program itself, from admissions through graduation, is carried on solely by the school. The agency's investment in the staff member is such that it remains interested in his development as a student while relinquishing his services as an employee during the time he is in attendance at school.

This division of responsibility may create difficulties, for instance when the agency recommends a staff member who may be turned down by the school's admissions department, or when a staff member, in his student role, does not do well in his field work or classes. But the freedom of the school must prevail in these delicate areas, and the agency cannot interfere except as it may wish to clarify standards and goals with the school. When the student returns to the agency between his first and second years at school as a summer employee, or after graduation, the agency must once again take on the responsibility for his further development as a worker, making every effort to help him integrate his professional education into his agency practice.

As an increasing number of public welfare personnel attend schools of social work, the task of the agency's staff development program will become more, and not less, challenging. For the returning graduate, the agency's practice will not appear as it did when he left for school. This will be particularly so if he has used his education well, for then he will be more sensitive and perceptive in many aspects of his job that once were familiar and routine.

For the graduate who is newly recruited to public welfare, his orientation will be an ongoing job for the first few months at least, but his training will be effective only if the agency has carved out a job for him that is appropriate to his new professional status and capacities. A professional worker in public welfare no longer need depend upon his civil service career; his education frees him to work in any social agency. Thus, the burden of making his job a challenging one rests with the agency. Professional education can ready the graduate, but like staff development it cannot serve as a substitute for appropriate tasks and enabling administration.

It is primarily through in-service training that the staff member will know what it means to provide services in public welfare, and the professional person will know this best. It is in the public welfare agency that the graduate will test his knowledge of the client and his total needs against a prepared budget; where he will use his new skills in method along with the standardized agency manual of practice; where he will want to provide services within the context of the agency's pressures of accountability. Yet, neither professional education nor in-service training are solutions for the social worker caught in dilemmas created by practical situations, any more than casework service is a solution for the problems of a client who is in need of money. The nature of the job, the salary he is paid, the conditions under which he works, and the validity of the service he performs will ultimately define the social worker's ability to sustain his competence.

The role of the graduate school is actually peripheral to the ongoing practice of the worker in public welfare. Training for certain aspects of this practice is essential, but education cannot compensate for questionable agency policies or restrictive programs. It is the function of staff development primarily to ready the worker for his job, to stimulate him toward creative practice, and to influence programs and policies so that the agency will retain the worker as long as possible.

Chapter Four

The Staff Development Process

Staff development, as a deliberate administrative process, grows out of the requirements of agency practice and the learning needs of staff. It is an over-all program related to the development of the practices of all staff—social service, clerical, and ancillary personnel—that directly or indirectly affect services to individuals, groups, or the community. Broadly defined, staff development may aim toward improving the attitudes of staff, encouraging them to think and make sound judgments, and supporting their desire to learn. It may be perceived as a contribution to staff retention, a countermovement to an emergency-ridden type of practice, a model of professional social work behavior, or an administrative effort to help staff in the difficult jobs they have to perform. More specifically defined, staff development may take place in supervision, administrative staff meetings, agency seminars, provision of educational leaves and scholarships, or use of the agency library.

Staff development in a social agency has an educational component, yet it differs from professional education. It has an administrative component, yet it differs in precise functions from the agency's administration. Staff development has the purpose of training staff so that practice is improved, the policies and program of the agency are carried out more effectively and its clients are better served.[1]

In-service training is one aspect of staff development, where skills are taught that are relevant to the tasks various workers are to perform, where knowledge of program, policies, and procedures is introduced to new staff members in their orientation period, and where selected content about clients and their problems and ways of helping them are taught in group or tutorial class sessions. While this teaching should be done conceptually to provide for the worker's integration and carry-over of learning from task to task, the scope of in-service training is essentially confined in its purpose, content, and materials to the specific agency function and the duties of the staff in question.

The method of staff development naturally derives from its aims and underlying premises. It is not the aim to inculcate expert professional knowledge, or to apply new ideas outside the context of the staff's experience. Beginning where the staff is, it should place its chief focus on the personnel's existing knowledge and skills, building slowly from that place to a level commensurate with the tasks to be accomplished. In other words, the method relies on the problems presented in daily practice; it does not reach for theory, but utilizes content derived from the staff's readily available experience. Learning takes place as the case is taught and as principles that devolve from it can be generalized for future practice. It is common that staff as well as administrative officers will expect the program to impart wisdom, but as we shall consider in a little greater detail later, this expectation is one of the subtle enticements that must be avoided if a staff development program is to be integrated with an ongoing, rigid, tradition-bound bureaucratic system. Wisdom can be easily rejected; intellectualization can be just as readily injected and spewed out, and new ideas, to the degree that they threaten existing ways of operating, can be easily misunderstood and misused.

Eileen Younghusband, in her brilliant report, *Training for Social Work,* has contributed two anecdotes which pointedly show "the dangers of teaching 'knowledge' concepts ahead of their being incorporated through use, understanding and attitude changes." [2] In the first an administrator meets a village level worker in a backward area and asks about his tenure and tasks there. The worker says he has been in the village for four months and has been collecting data:

"What about?" "Felt needs, sir." "What do you mean by felt needs?" "Mass approach, sir." "Mass approach method?" "Yes, psychological approach, sir."

The second anecdote has to do with a similar worker who is neatly dressed, carrying a notebook, and watching from afar a thousand people working on a community project. When asked by the administrator what he was doing there as an extension worker, the young man replied, "I am inspiring the people."

The point is that a staff development program must always be geared to where the staff is in its intellectual and emotional readiness, otherwise training will either signify words alone, or resistance will be raised to such a level that no teaching approach will be effective. The result of gearing training expectations thus is that it will take

longer, perhaps an indefinite time, for new ideas to be in-
culcated and integrated with ongoing practice; but in return there will be a receptivity and even excitement as the
staff gradually finds tolerance for the teacher and for the
content which at first may have appeared alien. It is at the
point where the predisposition of civil service staff and
professional content converge that the mutual threat
occurs. It doesn't matter if the content is excellent, and
well it might be. What matters is the willingness of the
staff to listen to it and to incorporate it into its practice.
Thus, staff development has to come to be seen as a state
of mind, readiness being a prerequisite to an experienced
working staff's capacity to examine its practice, to accept
new ideas, and to risk different ways of operating. It is
both essential and realistic to recognize the fact that new
ideas can be associated with professionalism, a situation
which naturally arouses the feeling that outsiders are
threatening the closed system.

Of course, a corollary to beginning where the staff is, is
the involvement of staff in all aspects of the program. As
people participate in a program they acquire an appreciation of it, an investment in its conduct and outcome,
which must necessarily propel them to help its cause.
Later we shall examine the ways in which this involvement can be demonstrated in a public welfare agency, and
the ways in which it can provide higher levels of staff in
the bureaucratic system with the opportunity to plan for
the program on lower levels, and even to teach in it. By
this method of engagement it becomes possible to develop
staff within the existing bureaucratic structure, disturbing
it as little as possible and yet affecting its functioning.

While the use of staff members as teachers and as curriculum planners may restrict somewhat the level of content and the outcome of the program, it offers advantages that far outweigh this disadvantage. When supervisory staff have full knowledge of the content being taught their workers, and when case supervisors assist in setting goals for their supervisors' workshops, their very participation provides ongoing support, if only because it removes the threat that a lower level of staff may come to know more than they. In a sense, the higher level of staff remains in charge although under direction of the staff development program.

This process appears unwieldy at times, because it is in itself staff development for the higher level of staff who in turn serve as the planning group or agency teachers. They become exposed to the new content they themselves will teach to others, and their obligation to impart this content will promote its absorption into their own thinking and practice. Furthermore, when higher levels take responsibility for defining the content and goals of in-service training sessions for their staff, they will care sufficiently to see that that training program is pursued. In other words, the total complement of personnel in public welfare will more readily become committed to staff development when the program is closely related to the existing and familiar hierarchical structure of the agency.

Beginning where the staff is, staying there as long as necessary, and striving for continued involvement of all levels in planning for their own learning, may suggest that a better quality of practice is not constantly held out to staff. This is not necessarily so; personnel in public welfare agencies, as well as people in other work situations and students at all levels, need continually to be confronted with ultimate aims and the outer boundaries of knowledge even though most goals may not be reached at once. This approach to staff development reflects a methodological concern arising from the need to lower resistance to learning in a group of people who are secure in their jobs yet are threatened by the inroads being made in their traditional ways of practicing. There may be short cuts to the process of staff development, but if the process of involvement is observed in some form it will more readily ensure that new ideas and sharpened skills will be accepted, integrated, and utilized by civil service personnel.

The only way to assure that efforts to reach staff will indeed reach them, is to observe a process that will ready them for new knowledge, prepare the way for the expression of their best attitudes, make it possible for them to make mistakes in the course of learning, and build in rewards to strengthen them. Without the participation of their superiors it is unlikely that any of these training aims will be supported, much less rewarded.

It would be folly not to recognize the restraints in this process for it is not only slow, it is also conserving of the system which in itself contains bureaucratic obstacles. Nevertheless, there seems to be little choice in the matter; personnel in a job setting are not students and they do not contract to learn, they contract to work. Many, in fact, have chosen work over schooling so as to avoid the pressures of education. Moreover, social service staff in a social agency, whether professionally trained or not, must spend most of their time while on their jobs performing their functions and tasks. Training is only one of the components of the agency's administrative program that enable workers to carry out their jobs, and because it is not an end in itself its chief criterion of effectiveness is the improvement of practice. A modified pace of training has the significant value of keeping in step with the agency's and the workers' practice limitations. If training moves ahead of practice it may well jeopardize the worker's immediate effectiveness.

It is only when the worker is on his job that we know the results of a staff development program and in-service training—when he is with his clients, and when he makes observations, judgments, and decisions that affect the client's life. Classroom behavior is an indicator of the student-worker's attitudes, intelligence, and competence, but as there is no test for these qualities except in the real life situation we can never be certain of them until the worker is in his practice and they can be evaluated. Teachers in professional schools can attest to this observation from their experience with classroom students who are amenable, bright, and scholarly but who, for any number of reasons, fail completely when they must apply knowledge through the screen of personality in the demanding practice situation. Conversely, it also happens that provocative, argumentative, and sullen classroom students may actually blossom in the field when they have responsibility for their own actions, and have greater compassion for their clients than they do for their teachers. Thus, the test of an effective staff development program is in the practice of the worker—not in the brilliance of the agency teacher, the pearls that may be strewn by a visiting scholar, the rich curriculum of study, the newest audio-visual aid equipment, or the platitudes of the staff development planners.

It is well known that the acquisition of knowledge for use takes place through the application of that knowledge. In social agencies, at any rate, an educationally oriented type of supervision helps to make known the meaning and relationship between knowledge and practice. In a staff development program, as in a school of social work, formal classroom teaching of concepts and principles must always be taught within the framework of practice that is ongoing and familiar to the worker. One of the major differences between field work that is part of social work educational experience, and the daily practice of a social worker in a public welfare agency, is that the former is educational in aim and method, and the latter is completely job-oriented. Under the pressures and emergencies that characterize the practice experience of the public welfare worker, there is limited room or time for development of a sequence of learning so that the worker may learn from the simple and move on to the complex. There is little opportunity in a public welfare agency that has uncovered caseloads, which are partially due to open intake policies and personnel shortages, for the worker to have selected learning experiences and the chance to apply theory. We must always question whether even the finest in-service training program with the richest theoretical content can be integrated with the worker's practice when the practice itself is disorganized and the worker so overwhelmed that he cannot recognize the connection between what he learned in the morning and what he is doing on his job in the afternoon. One common result of this conflict is frustration and anger on the part of the worker. One of the ways in which integration can be accomplished is by gearing the classroom learning situation to the practice situation in staff development, as opposed to the reverse way, in which education ideally takes place in a professional school of social work.

Again we observe a restraint in the process, because the public welfare worker cannot be expected primarily to achieve educational purposes in his practice. If there were such a concept as work purposes, this would serve as a more apt description of the worker's practice. Contradictions evident in the "right" way as taught in the agency classroom situation versus the "wrong" way as practiced perforce by the hard-pressed worker functioning in an imperfect situation could create a serious conflict of interests, rather than an integration of learning. Therefore, a wiser choice lies in the direction of adapting the classroom content to the practice experience. This, in its fullest meaning, is "beginning where the staff is." Case illustrations, problems to be considered, supporting knowledge, and method itself—all must derive from the worker's daily practice; in one way or another his experiences can guide the basic curriculum of the in-service training program. The worker's experiences may be expanded into governing principles, they may be explored with him as representing theory, they may be compared with other ways of practice, but always the content to be taught should reflect what the worker is doing. That is the way of in-service training in a social agency; first the jobs must be done, and the meanings found later.

What is the role of the immediate supervisor in this type of learning situation? The supervisor naturally must have the responsibility for the worker's practice, administratively and educationally. It is the supervisor who is present and on the spot, who knows the caseload, who has access to administrative supports and limitations of the worker's practice; it is the supervisor who knows, and is known best by, the worker. It would seem, therefore, that the supervisor is the primary source of learning as well as control of the untrained worker in practice in a public welfare agency. In view of the importance of this role, let us return to the image of a well-turned-out staff development program, supported perhaps by federal funds, employing a commanding staff of professional social workers, all with teaching experience and able to utilize all of the resources for training in the agency and the community, including extension courses in the local school of social work. The presence of such a training staff in the program would surely be a reflection of the agency's interest in promoting the learning of its practitioner staff. However, it is a fact that the professional personnel of the staff development program never have as close a connection with the workers as do the supervisors.

How then can good practice habits be taught, particularly if the supervisory staff in the agency are the very ones who have been employed there the longest and may be the most tradition-bound group in the agency as far as practice is concerned? According to our conception of staff development as a process which must begin where staff are and involve them in all aspects of the program, there is no choice but to accept the fact that the supervisors of practice are the core group to which in-service training must be directed. They are the ones who stay the longest, the crucial people when it comes to direct work with practitioners, the ones who know the agency's program the best. They are the permanent foundation of the agency. That the agency's program pivots on the supervisory group is particularly evident when the workers are untrained and transitory, and when case supervisors and other administrative staff are involved in keeping the bureaucracy going.

It has to be recognized that these characteristics of the first-line supervisors are the very ones that make it difficult to work with them. They often are not young, and usually have risen on the promotional ladder without professional education. Ordinarily they have an authority that stems from direct knowledge of the caseloads and the workers, to an extent that no other level of staff has in the agency. They are indispensable as is no other group to the ongoing work of public welfare. Therefore, it is obvious that the influence of the staff development program needs to be felt first by the supervisors if the program is to be effective.

The educational function of the supervisor is particularly crucial with respect to the untrained social work technician. Such a worker must have someone to tell him what to do and, perhaps equally important, to tell him what he *has done* so that intellectual connections will take place and learning will be transferred to later experiences. This is the educational component of supervision that points to the difference between when a social work technician is doing a routine job and performing tasks perfunctorily, and when he is deriving meaning and gratification from his practice. The supervisor is the only person under the hierarchical system found in most bureaucratic public welfare agencies who has sufficient access to the worker to help him find that meaning.

In-service training really rests, then, with the supervisor and not with the administrative unit of staff development

personnel. The efforts of a staff development progi
need to be directed to the enhancement of the supervisc
teaching skills, his knowledge of practice, and his constructive attitudes. Indirect as it may seem, the most direct way to affect the welfare of the client group is
through training the supervisor of the worker who deals
with the client.

Before expanding our discussion of the programmatic
aspects of staff development, its method and content, a
word ought to be said about the allusion just made to
interrupting the bureaucratic structure as little as possible. Analysts of social structure caution us, with good
reason, about the problems inherent in large bureaucratic
organizations. Dimock, for example, has commented
sagely on the inflexibilities and red tape that result from
size alone, and the concomitant rigidities that occur in
hierarchical organizations.[3] The stratifications existing in
staff organization make for what Dimock calls "improper
staff activity" and centralized staff controls that create
timidity. The inherent job security of a civil service staff
contributes to the introversion and conservatism of the
group, making new ideas competitive with the reigning
mediocrity that inevitably derives from the status
granted to seniority, tradition, and conformance. For
where there is such a closed system, change can be upset-
ting to the surrounding comforts of familiar rules and
regulations; tested procedures carry greater weight in the
daily activities of the staff than do current theories about
their work.

In the light of the restrictions upon effective practice in
large, highly specialized bureaucratic organizations, how
then can we conceive of any program to fit into this sys-

tem? The outlines of such a program as just described would certainly promote the negative result of a "pecking order" for, in a sense, what we really are subscribing to as a value is that higher levels of staff be the chief carriers of the training message to lower levels.

In partial explanation of this position, it is important to note that since hierarchical personnel arrangements and bureaucratic constrictions are in fact realities of public welfare organization, no form of staff development program alone will change or even very much affect this structure. If there is any question in the reader's mind about the effect of a single program or a single person upon a bureaucratic organization, he need only observe the results evident in a public welfare agency where new service amendments to old legislation have been introduced, or where a professional social worker has become a chief administrator, commissioner, or staff development consultant. While these innovations in a particular agency may be all to the good for the present and future of the welfare program, none of the supposed advantages brought by higher standards will have as significant an impact upon the staff of a highly bureaucratic agency as will the announcement of a promotional examination or a civic award to a staff member. A closed system of personnel is a force in itself, a going concern, as it were, and not a family or a loosely knit social group. A civil service staff is not easily enticed by transient people in power; the apolitical nature of civil service provides for continuity of personnel, whether a new mayor is elected or a new social work practice is promoted. The incumbent staff will continue to function as before unless it can be convinced of the usefulness of new ways of operating. Social work practice ordinarily is not improved through edict, for attitudes do not change automatically in the wake of new social legislation. A public welfare staff that has not enjoyed the respect of the agency administration and has been without appropriate social work models of behavior will observe only the letter of the law, unless there is a concomitant willingness on the part of staff to adapt its familiar practices to new approaches.

The 1962 amendments to the Public Welfare Law provide for preventive services, but neither the law nor response to authority will induce the social worker to observe a family's need for some vital household necessity when the family itself is afraid to request it. The worker may check his list and may follow his directions because he is well adapted to his bureaucratic role, but only when he is concerned with client need will he recognize its existence in many disguised forms. It is only his compassionate attitude that will permit a family to confide in him, and only his conviction that will impel him to press the agency for the service or the money he finds necessary. These attitudinal characteristics are not touched by legislation or administrative fiat, nor are they much affected by logic. Yet they are the very approaches that need to be brought about through an effective staff development program.

The fact remains that it is the hierarchical system that is meaningful for public welfare staff; it is this structure that provides promotional opportunities for careerists in civil service, and thus commands respect. We are not concerned here with an evaluation of bureaucracy, but are only preoccupied with the problem of how to influence, constructively and democratically, the institutionalized staff of a bureaucratic public welfare agency. To the degree that we accept the reality of the function of a bureaucracy and come to terms with the gratifications it holds for staff, it will become evident that there are few, if any, other choices left open to us. Moreover, the fact that there are good as well as bad effects of bureaucratic influences upon staff practice suggests that there are strengths within the structure, and it is these that we propose to call upon in our exposition of the process of staff development. The following finding summarized by Peter M. Blau, in his well-known study of staff attitudes toward clients in a public welfare agency, exemplifies this point:

A study of a public welfare agency indicated that bureaucratic constraints became internalized and thus limited service to clients. But adaptation to bureaucratic procedures lessened rigidity and thus promoted casework service. Many newcomers experienced a "reality shock," to which they often reacted by losing interest in the welfare of clients. For integrated workers, however, social support from colleagues absorbed the impact of this reality shock.[4]

Another justification for merging a staff development process into an ongoing bureaucratic structure rather than placing it in juxtaposition to it, is that of maintaining a necessary equilibrium in the state of things. Whether for humanitarian reasons, expedience, or because it is just sound administrative practice, a program (or an administrator, teacher, social worker, or doctor) must not seek to undermine an existing equilibrium unnecessarily. The effects of doing so may range from discomfort to anarchy, and in a democratic society one cannot justify manipulative methods to achieve even high social aims. A "body" of staff, just like a human body, requires its homeostatic balance in order to sustain itself. Interruption in the order of things demands that something else be built in to take the place of the disruption, or the organism will falter. This is a natural phenomenon which staff development planners would be wise to observe.

A dramatic, if mundane, example will illustrate this necessity either to maintain a balance of forces or to build in supports where the balance is disrupted. The reader is undoubtedly familiar with the emphasis placed upon paper work in public welfare agencies. Some of this, of course, is essential for purposes of accountability and administration in a complex organization, and some of it is unnecessary. The requirement of excessive paper work may reflect the administration's uncertainty or a lack of confidence in lower levels of staff, or it may be the inevitable outcome of overcentralization of administrative functions. Whether or not the paper work is essential to the work of the agency is not to be our concern here. What is significant is that too often the wrong people must take care of it. This function should be the charge of clerical staff, but it is well known that it often character-izes a marked proportion of the social worker's job as well. Lately, the field of public welfare has undertaken a long overdue change in this state of affairs. The cry is abroad that clerks should do the job they are trained for and do best, and that social workers should be saved for direct and supporting work with clients.

In one public welfare agency an experiment was under-taken to see what would happen when clerical tasks were returned to appropriate personnel. It had long been a major complaint of the social service staff that they had too much paper work to do, and in order to determine if the release of this work would improve the quantity and quality of their service to clients, the administration permitted them to give up filling out certain forms, or rather to arrange for clerks to fill them out. No additional training was provided for the social work staff in support of this new program emphasis, but functions were reallocated and time was found for social work tasks. Staff was simply relieved of some clerical duties, and the result was near-chaos. Workers could be seen at secretarial typewriters showing clerks how to fill out the forms, and new forms were devised to assure that the old forms would be preserved. The effect upon service to clients was not noticeable, as the workers did not utilize the newly found time to do more for them; rather, they found more desk work to do, even if this meant merely cleaning out drawers. One worker was even discovered writing out her dictation in longhand instead of dictating it into a machine as she had done before.

Why did this phenomenon occur? The social work staff was sincere in its dislike of clerical work, but this function had become institutionalized as a way of life, as indeed had the staff's complaints about it. Moreover, with no guidelines for using the additional time constructively, the workers foundered. More significantly, the availability of additional time placed greater demands upon their social work skills, and made apparent to them and to their superiors the real paucity of their practice knowledge and competence. No longer could they feel that they might have accomplished more if only they had not had other demands on their time.

Finally, a factor that did not prove to be extraneous was that in the heavy pressure of the public welfare day, whether in the field or in the office, the workers simply had to have a change of pace, an outlet that was legitimate and yet not as demanding as continually interviewing clients. Taking care of the paper work part of service to clients provided this outlet. A less ambitious staff with lower morale might have turned to the daily newspaper, excessive coffee breaks, or other illegitimate devices. The carrying out of paper work tasks requires little energy for an intelligent social worker; in any event, until the time of the experiment it enabled the worker to round out his day by fulfilling his obligations to the agency and to the clients, with no complicating factor of guilt to contend with.

This example of the interruption of a bureaucratic process without accompanying supports—in this case training—illustrates what can happen when balance is disrupted and no effort is made to compensate for the inevitable "shock" to the system. This is a pitfall our process of staff development will attempt to avoid. Overteaching may well be more disruptive than underteaching when the actual experience of the worker in the agency does not reflect the content or method of the teaching. The immediate goals of staff development in public welfare must be fairly conservative if the program is to remain in step with the total agency operation. The ultimate aim, however, is not to retain the status quo, but to affect it positively, to change it from the old to the new, from whatever it was to whatever it may become. The rub is that this aim cannot be achieved through fiat, through "vitamin shots," or through imitation. A process of integration must be observed in order not to lose the support of staff while advancing toward the objective. Slow and restrained though it is, this process will provide for the necessary self-containment, and maintain the equilibrium, of a staff working in a highly organized bureaucratic structure.

Before we examine how this may be done, we must concern ourselves with one further element in the process—the staff trainer or staff development consultant and the role he is to play in the structure. This is a vital matter and is becoming increasingly so as federal funds are being made available to states and communities for the hiring of competent personnel to provide leadership in staff development programs. Often this leadership is defined as educational *cum* administrative in character. The staff development person is conceived of as part teacher and part chief administrator, a person in a special staff, as opposed to a traditional line, position—a purveyor of wisdom and a bearer of standards. He is perceived as filling all of these roles, but as being without full administrative authority.

As though this definition of his job were not clouded enough, the staff development person is also thought of as a suprapractitioner, while not in direct practice; a scholar, while not a faculty person in the academic sense; a competent, well-known, efficient, social worker, yet one who is willing to work in an agency that barely accepts his talents or is outright hostile to him. Often he is expected to have had wide professional experience outside the agency, and yet to be a part of the staff itself, having gone up the promotional ladder within the very agency setting.

Contradictory as these qualifications may appear to be, they describe a commonly held image of the staff development person. In a very real sense he must be all these things, or come as close as possible to the model. In line with our conception of the staff development process, it would be most congenial to perceive the person in charge as a consultant. A consultant in a social service agency is essentially an enabler, not a practitioner, supervisor, or administrator. As a consultant he can fit into any of the hierarchical levels since he carries no administrative authority. His repertory derives from his competence as a teacher; his authority rests in his knowledge. He will be expected to establish a role that encompasses full knowledge of the agency and its relationships with the welfare superstructure and the community. He will need to know its function, program, policies, traditions, and hidden as well as overt paths of communication. In addition to these specifics, he will have to bring with him to this terrifying job the competence of his professional knowledge about people and of psychosocial, cultural, economic, and biological phenomena, as well as knowledge about social work methods and how to communicate them. At the same time, as he learns to know the staff intimately, he must remain always on the perimeter of involvement in the actual practice of the agency, for his effectiveness lies in the development of staff, not in his direct participation in their practice, supervision, or administration.

The direct activities of the consultant are contained within the structure of the program as defined by the agency's functions and its particular staff needs. Those activities are usually concerned with the development of teaching materials, the organization and conduct of workshops and other in-service training groups, consultation with those on staff who may lead the groups, as well as actual teaching in some instances. The indirect activities of the consultant may, on the other hand, comprise the larger component of his job. They are somewhat obscure and undefined when examined out of context, but they are manifold as they reach out into all areas of the agency's program. So long as the consultant is administratively related to the highest officer in the agency, his impact upon staff practice will be felt in matters of hiring and firing, personnel policies, educational leave arrangements, questions of staff control, and always in the problem of staff morale. The list is endless, and tends to find its limitations or boundaries in accordance with the acceptance of the consultant by the administrator and by the staff with whom the consultant works. As Merton has said:

The earlier in the continuum of decision that the bureaucratic intellectual operates, the greater his potential influence in guiding the decision. . . . More typically, however, the bureaucratic individual finds himself in a position where he is called upon to provide information for alternative or specific policies which have already been formulated by policy makers. . . . When problems reach this stage in the continuum of the decision, he comes to think largely in instrumental terms and to accept the prevailing definitions of objectives. His perspectives are fixed accordingly.[5]

In the light of this learned observation on policy making in a public welfare agency, the caution to the staff development consultant is clear enough. He must somehow be in a position to participate in decision making, and his job should be placed high enough in the structure for this participation to be effective. Yet, in order to reach the staff on whose learning problems he is to work, he must be mobile and, to the extent possible, be *of* them. For if the consultant remains entrenched with the chief administrator, effective though he may be in this role, he will become in the eyes of the staff not only a suspected outsider but also one of the "bosses." The lot of the consultant in staff development, like that of the policeman, is not a happy one.

Chapter Five

Orientation and Training
of Newly Hired Staff

We noted in a previous chapter that the average turnover of social service staff in public welfare agencies throughout the country runs from 20 to 26 percent annually. Inevitably this means that agencies will have a large replacement rate, and as caseloads in public welfare must have continuous coverage, usually it is necessary for the agencies to hire new staff almost immediately. For the reader who may not have experienced the pressures caused by staff vacancies, it may seem like a casual problem to hire personnel, when it is available, at the times necessary. But for a staff development program this form of hiring creates a logistical training problem of no small dimension.

To take an example realistic in the extreme, let us consider the hiring situation in a large urban public welfare agency. In a staff of 500 child welfare workers, let us say, a turnover rate of 20 percent a year would mean that 100 new staff would have to be hired annually to replace those who leave their jobs through resignation, retirement, promotion, or educational leave. While it would not be entirely accurate to divide this number by the twelve months of the year, since there are pressure turnover periods like the early fall and late spring, let us imagine that each month there are staff vacancies numbering ten workers. In a public assistance program where there may be 2,000 workers and a turnover rate of 25 percent the hiring rate would be about 50 a month. These figures of course would not account for additional staff required for any program expansion.

A decision on the manner of hiring must be made administratively, and here the influence of the consultant in staff development should be felt with an impact. In a period of pressure, particularly, an agency will want every staff member for whom a budget line exists, so that its program may be carried out effectively. In the light of this requirement, hiring may occur at any time there is a vacancy, perhaps at the rate of one or two workers a day, three a week, or ten a month. Filling vacant positions immediately would seem like a reasonable administrative plan. But what of the training of the new workers? Can scattered hiring provide for an organized program of training, particularly if any part of that training is to be centered on group instruction? What of the strain upon supervisors who may have one or more workers entering units at various times in the year, all needing the same orientation to the job? What of the workers who must enter the complex world of public welfare alone, without a group with which to identify? An administrator who entertains these questions may well consider holding the hiring periods to an annual, semiannual, or even monthly basis, depending upon the needs of his program and the willingness of the incumbent staff to cover extra caseloads. As for this latter point, staff will often be willing to do this rather than to tolerate the confusion of initiating new members continually throughout the year.

A word needs to be said here about crash training programs, which often appear as solutions to the dilemma facing public welfare agencies when staff are needed and there is no time to train them effectively. The notion of a crash training program is reminiscent of the pressure upon graduate schools to train social workers in a hurry, to scale down their education but nonetheless to train them well. It would seem that if it were at all possible to compress the professional education experience or the in-service training program of public welfare staff, this would be done to the relief of all concerned. However, learning, whether in a school or on the job, does not happen in a "crash"; it requires time for materials to be taught, and, perhaps more important, time for these materials to be integrated, digested, and applied by the student or the worker. Since in-service training in a public welfare agency is usually directed toward enabling the social worker to modify his attitudes and to operate fairly independently, it must be remembered that the task of training is to strengthen the worker's powers of observation and judgment, to provide him with the necessary tools to carry out his job by himself. This is a very different matter from the kind of short cut method used to teach a machinist to run a lathe or a soldier to speak Chinese.

The level of content and the use to which it is to be put determines the method and timing of the teaching. In order to make a crash training program really effective, it would be necessary to change the aims of in-service training in public welfare agencies. This possibility suggests a choice in itself, but it is far less of a choice in this decade, in the shadow of the service amendments, than it was previously when the program of public welfare agencies was more limited in scope. Earlier, a worker in public assistance could have been trained efficiently, in a very short time, to determine the financial need of a family according to a prepared budget schedule. Moreover, in the days when child placement was seen as a better plan, *a priori*, than keeping the child with his own family, a child welfare worker might have been easily and quickly trained to place children perfunctorily and without evaluation. The developments in knowledge and in the social legislation that reflects that knowledge have narrowed the choices open to administrators, as far as the aims of training are concerned.

Frankly put, if the aims of public welfare lie in the prevention of social breakdown and in rehabilitation from social dysfunction, then social work staff must be trained to undertake the complex tasks involved. Clearly, it is not enough to affirm one's convictions about the necessity of training; it is imperative to give the training a chance to work. Crash training programs are a mockery and really have no place in a respectable staff development program in public welfare. More firmly stated, perhaps it would be better to expose the new worker to no training at all rather than to lower his sights so quickly in the game and give him the impression that crash practice is all the agency will want of him. Above all, in the long run it is to be expected that an effective training program would play a large part in any agency's efforts to retain staff, and would reduce the turnover rate that creates an apparent need for a crash program.

When new social workers are hired at reasonable periods and in manageable groups that are not too small or too large, the in-service training program may begin its task. The matter of the size of the group is very difficult to discuss out of context. There is no magical number that makes a group just right, and much would depend upon the content of the in-service training program and the size of the agency. In a large urban agency that is accustomed to the hurly-burly of huge numbers of workers, sometimes running to the thousands, the incumbent staff would hardly notice an incoming group of twenty-five workers. On the other hand, in a small agency of twenty-five social workers it is obvious that a single new worker would make an impression, and a training group of five would be more in keeping with the pace and scope of the agency.

Recalling that in-service training of newly hired social work personnel is but one part of the staff development process in a public welfare agency, and that this process requires the participation of the total staff in some form or other, we can see that the conduct of the training program should, of course, be woven into the general fabric of the total staff. Thus, the incumbent staff should know about the presence of the new group who will shortly be sharing its quarters, and it follows that those responsible for the supervision of the new workers should know exactly what is being taught to them in preparation for their coming on the actual job. For the sake of both new and old employees, it is a major task of the staff development program to establish and maintain this communication.

Another caution to be kept in mind is that the in-service training program for newly hired staff resembles not at all the induction of new students in a graduate school of social work. All this has been stated before, but at this point where we are considering an agency program about to embark on its course of training, it is crucial to reiterate one significant difference. The newly hired social worker is at the brink of a job experience, not an educational one, as is his academic colleague. Whether the training period is to go on for one week or six months, the new worker's objective, and surely the objective of the agency, is that he get to his job, not that he become learned in the social work profession. Again, the administrator and the staff development consultant are confronted with a number of choices, some of which have greater merit than others.

There are patterns of training programs which take the newly hired worker away to the seclusion of an agency-based institute of training for a specified period of time. This form of program is more applicable in a rural area where distances are great and the state training personnel must address themselves at one time to groups of trainees collected from five or six small county offices. It has greater justification in this case than in an urban center where an agency would undoubtedly have a sufficient number of trainees to comprise a group in a single neighborhood office. Yet this pattern is often observed in an urban agency as well. It might be of some value to ponder the reasons for its popularity, for it does indeed seem to hold particular value.

There are many examples of this kind of training program, most of which employ a competent staff of teachers and often use an entire building or several floors. The usual pattern is that the newly hired staff of a county, state, or local agency are asked to report first to this installation for orientation, training, and ultimately for assignment to their jobs. The training staff are, perhaps, perceived as faculty, the new workers as students, and the course of study is referred to as the curriculum. The academic flavor is at once obvious, and quite possibly it is preferred for reasons of status, at least for the staff involved. It is not irrelevant to note that often the training staff of this kind of program are drawn from the agency itself, even though the consultant in staff development or the training chief may be recruited from outside. It is understandable that this new status is a cherished role for training staff, who have spent much of their career in the highly pressured atmosphere of the public welfare agency, and even if it may not be viewed as a promotion for a staff person to become a "faculty member," it certainly relieves him of the more burdensome requirements of his previous job. This is not to suggest that in-service training is easy and without its own demands. Rather, it is obvious that an in-service training function, much like a teaching job, carries with it certain characteristic elements of quiet, if not serenity, and of protection from emergency-laden cases, if not academic freedom.

This very distance from the job may please the training staff but at the same time have a deleterious effect upon the program, for the training staff may then lose sight of many of the aspects of the work environment. It should be the aim of the training program to initiate the newly hired staff into the ongoing practices of the agency, regardless of what those practices may be. Naturally, practices that are not conducive to staff development should be modified, otherwise there is no point to an elaborate in-service training program. If the desks are placed too close together in the agency proper, what is the value of introducing the new worker to a setting where he has a private office, or even reasonable space? If the noise is deafening in the agency, how will the new worker become accustomed to it if he spends his first weeks in the unreal quiet atmosphere of a training institute? If supervisors are short-tempered because the pressure of work is so extreme, how will the patient, accepting attitudes of the training staff prepare workers for the kind of supervision in store for them? If the caseloads to which they will address themselves are full of severe social pathology, how ready will the new workers be for the real job if in training they carry only cases selected for their simplicity?

A final concern, in considering the commitment to total involvement of staff in the training of workers, is that while a high level of training may be going on in the institute, the rest of the incumbent staff, most importantly the supervisors of the new workers, may remain uninvolved in the program of training.

When the new workers move into their jobs, it often happens that the supervisors train them again, in their way. This induction process may take equally as long as the training institute program, and usually it is effected unofficially, without the involvement of the training staff. The response of the worker who is caught in the middle of this double training program is inevitably one of frustration. Is he to believe the kindly training staff that told him he should listen well to his client so as to form a relationship and enlist his cooperation in a program of self-fulfillment? Or is he to pay attention to his supervisor, who may or may not approve of what the worker learned in the training institute but will often feel impelled to say, "Yes, yes, that is right, but we must get on with it and you really are spending too much time at your home visits, etc., etc." A newly hired worker has only one of two courses of action available to him under such circumstances; he will leave the agency which has caught him in the "double bind," or he will accede to the demands of his supervisor, as he is the authority to whom he absolutely must relate during his term as a worker.

Of course, some workers will return to the training institute to chat with the staff and tell them of the troubles in the agency. But their reports are not likely to change the situation. Because of the isolation of the training staff from the work environment, they cannot affect a supervisor's attitude, nor can they be in the slightest way helpful to the new worker who has graduated to his job. This unfortunate phenomenon is a logical result of removing the training staff from the mainstream of agency practice.

The training institute is an extreme example of a common kind of training program in this country. Its separateness cannot help but insulate it from the agency's real pressures and real learning problems. As it remains separate it trains to a greater or less degree for the agency's practice, but it really is not *of* the agency. It might well be a small-scale, imitation school of social work, which holds no pretense of training for the work of a particular agency. It is in the image of the training institute that we can observe the supposedly important training advances being made. Newly hired staff may be exposed to the highest level of training, they may have a complete beginning social work library, a course of study that is of the highest professional standard, and teachers who are competent and dedicated. This form of training program is the kind that will be noticed by the budget examiner and the federal field worker, because it has substance and clarity. The questions for us to ponder here are whether or not it works as in-service training; whether it prepares workers for the job as it is, not as we would wish it to be; whether it promotes constructive working relationships between the new staff and the incumbent staff.

There is another drawback to the institute as a form of training for newly hired staff, particularly where the bulk of the training effort is placed upon it. That is that where such a program has become literally institutionalized, and where large numbers of new people are trained each year, the greatest effort of the agency's training program is expended upon new staff, many of whom will remain only a short period of time and consequently will have the least impact of any group upon the total program of the agency. Thus the staff development program rapidly becomes an orientation program for new staff even though it is apparent that there are other important functions for it to perform.

True, the training institute often houses programs of ongoing training, sometimes called refresher courses, for incumbent staff on all levels. Again, it must be noted that these programs must have the same disadvantages as the induction program we have just described. The isolation from the agency does not make for a strong program of in-service training for the senior staff and supervisors. Patterns of resistance are developed, and the content remains insular. For the time the worker spends away from his job in such a training institute, he might better attend a local school of social work where he can receive a course of instruction that has been thought through by academic specialists and taught by professional teachers.

Keeping in mind our view of staff development and professional education as discrete processes, let us now return to our conception of in-service training for newly hired staff under the auspices of a staff development program that is appropriately integrated into the bureaucratic life of the agency.

A feasible program of in-service training for newly hired social workers was attempted in one large urban public welfare agency in both the public assistance and child welfare departments, and it had a core of effectiveness for a number of reasons.[1] As we shall see, the program to be discussed contained the features essential to meeting the multiple administrative and educational demands of staff development. That is, the work of the agency was carried on, at least minimally, by the new staff members themselves almost immediately upon their first appearance at the agency. At the same time, the new workers remained in a protected work situation for a period of time that could be extended or contracted in accordance with the pressures upon the agency to hire and train additional staff. The third characteristic of this plan was that it observed the process we have elaborated on previously, where supervisors play the chief role in the training of their workers.

For lack of a better designation we shall call this the *training unit plan* for newly hired social workers. Among the ways in which it differs from the training institute plan just described is that the new staff are assigned immediately to active units within the mainstream of the agency, and their supervisors do the actual training on the job, using the new workers' actual caseloads. This type of training experience becomes one of gradual adaptation to the demands of the agency, including that of relating to a variety of colleagues as well as of building a full caseload within a prescribed period of time. When the training in these units is accomplished there is no need to reintroduce the new staff into the life of the agency; furthermore, they are prepared for the impact of the full caseload and the disordered life of the agency, because they have been gradually introduced rather than catapulted into it. The worker, arriving with a group of people as new as he is and staying on with a small unit of this group, can sustain the important relationships he needs in order to cope with what Blau has called "reality shock."

The role of the supervisor, in this instance the training supervisor, is crucial to the induction and training of the new worker. Training supervisors with teaching skills and interest in the program can be enlisted for the task, and the number required will, of course, depend upon the rate of hiring and the size of existing units. These supervisors, involved as they are in the staff development program and fully participating in the training process, would naturally be in the best position to carry out the educational purposes of the program, and would always be closely connected with the conduct of whatever larger group training was also going on in the agency. As the training supervisors become the core of the agency's teaching staff, they themselves can participate in a variety of forms of in-service training by learning methods of supervision, being brought up to date on new materials, and by numerous other means.

The presence of training units in a public welfare agency relieves the bulk of staff from the coming and going of brand new workers; it confines the hustle and bus-

tle that accompanies uncertainty to the training unit itself,
leaving the remaining units free to do their work. This,
incidentally, is one of the compensating factors for incumbent staff as they carry the greater weight of the caseloads
during the initial period of the new workers' training. Due
to its flexibility, this plan has other administrative advantages. Training units do not need to be restricted to a special setting in the agency, but if this is desirable they may
be. The units may be organized in a relatively quiet center or in a busy, emergency-ridden program of the agency.
They may be spread among divisions or departments, or
they may be placed in a selected program. If there is time,
that is if newer staff do not have to be hired right away,
the training units can go on indefinitely, certainly up to a
year. On the other hand, if the turnover rate is such that
newer staff must be hired quickly, one or more than one of
the existing training units can be disbanded after a few
months. The units are not necessarily tied to each other,
except as all the new workers may participate in an additional simultaneous group training program, the content
of which would be supported in the trainee's practice in
his unit.

The protected, and to some extent protracted, learning
experience thus provided for newly hired social workers
inevitably results in more judicious practice during and
after training. The atmosphere itself provides the opportunity for workers to ask more questions and to think
through the tasks they are learning. Their responses to the
clients they serve is less routine, and they are undoubtedly less frantic about the job confronting them, and so
more orderly in their management of it. When young college graduates apply for a job in a public welfare agency

they are usually enthusiastic about handling their first case and meeting their first client. It seems only fair to them that the agency's training program support this enthusiasm by immediately providing the chance to become active on the caseload. "Immediately" may be the first day at the agency or the third, but surely not too long after the worker's arrival.

In the first place, the anxiety built up by the new employee about the unknown experience in store for him would be much more trying than the initial fear of carrying out his first social work effort. In the second place, it must be kept in mind that the real world of work in the public welfare agency has pressures of all kinds, and the new worker should begin to be exposed rapidly to this reality. He may even be less stunned by it at the beginning, because he probably will not be sufficiently knowledgeable to recognize the host of painful problems to be brought to him by his clients.

As we are always interested in couching the educational experience of the new worker in administrative terms, a word should be spoken in favor of the time-saving aspect of training units. Materials can be taught once to a group rather than several times, as they must be when new staff members are added to the ongoing unit of incumbent workers. The fact that all members of the training unit are on the same level of knowledge and experience suggests that some of the learning can be shared, and that the workers can learn from each other as well as from their training supervisor and the other agency people who are responsible for their job indoctrination.

The training unit plan, above all its other characteristics, has one quality in particular that makes it advantageous. It is one aspect of the staff development program that is *of* the natural life of the agency. It receives no more and no less attention than it requires, and as it flows into the agency's total practice it remains self-contained while not provoking resistance from incumbent staff or administrators.

When a training unit program like the one just described was tried in a public welfare agency, it had one serious drawback which probably will not have to exist as long as federal funds continue to be available for the training of staff. The training supervisors were drawn from the regular complement of staff and not from new budget lines. The program would be even more feasible and less disrupting if an agency were to have extra training supervisors added to the normally budgeted positions.

The matter of orientation of newly hired staff is significant enough as part of the ongoing in-service training program of a public welfare agency, but often it is perceived as the major task of training. According to the dictionary, orientation means "Determination or sense of one's position with relation to environment or to some particular person, thing, field of knowledge, etc." [2] This suggests that the orientation period for a new staff member would not take very long, perhaps a day or two at the very most. It means that the worker must be introduced to the relevant things in the situation in which he will later receive training. What are these things? For one thing, a brief— necessarily brief at first—description of what the agency does, and most important what the worker himself will be expected to do. It is he who is the focal subject of the orientation, not the aims of the agency, the concerns of the community, or the problems of the clientele. It is he who must adapt to the strange situation in which he finds himself. From his point of view he may be primarily interested at the moment in where the rest room is, where and when he will have lunch, who the speaker is, how he will be trained, the working hours, and when he will get paid. In his effort to establish a role at the very beginning, there is very little else the new worker will hear or take in during his period of orientation. He will not be able to absorb the most brilliant description of the history of the agency and he will inevitably be deaf to any discussion at all of policies and procedures that do not affect his immediate situation, which is usually related to personnel matters. Often, a welcoming address by an important person in the agency can be uplifting to the new worker, particularly if it is focused upon him and his value to the agency and its program.

In this description of an orientation period there is no hint of training. It is true that very often what is not known about the job by the new worker is appalling, but all he is ready for is to find out where his desk is to be. An ambitious, well-intended in-service training program will be concerned with major issues in social welfare, the organization of the agency, and even the nature of society and humanity, but these issues might not involve the worker until he sees his first case and is helped to derive larger meanings from it. It has been the experience of many a teacher that the first class is often lost as far as reaching the students with the content is concerned, even though it sets the tone for the remainder of the semester and gives the teacher and the students a chance to look each other over. There must, of course, be a first session, but the expectations of this session have to be geared to the real situation. A casual atmosphere and sufficient opportunity for the worker to ask questions will set the tone and will ready the worker for what is to come.

The goal then for the orientation period for new workers is not to teach what is better learned in small doses under conditions favorable to education, spaced according to practice needs. Rather, it is to acquaint the worker with the most superficial aspects of his job, not so that he will learn them at once, but so that when he goes home that first night, thinks about the job, and tells his family what happened during the day, he will be glad he made the decision to go to work at the agency. The sooner he is assigned a desk, a supervisor, a caseload, and carefully defined tasks, the sooner he will learn by doing. It is then that his initial anxiety will be replaced by the activity and excitement of learning and achieving.

We have now almost launched the newly hired worker on his way upon the mainstream of the work of the public welfare agency. Once oriented and assigned to his training unit, he has yet to participate in the more structured group teaching sessions. We shall call this *central training* to distinguish it from the learning that goes on in training units. At this juncture we should again consider the administrative choices involved in the kind of a training program we are examining. There will be an extra investment of time and cost, because the workers will have to be relieved of their job duties and often will have to use time to travel as well to attend central training sessions. When the choice to adopt the central training program is made it must be recognized that blocks of time will be needed, organized by the staff development consultant toward a sequence of learning. This may mean two hours a week for six weeks, or one hour every other day for two or three weeks. The way in which this part of the program is planned is not at issue here. The significant point is that there must be sufficient time available to achieve reasonable training objectives. An adequate number of well-spaced central training sessions interspersed with the practical work of the training units is necessary for the workers' learning, testing out, and integration of important content. During the induction period there can be no substitute for the time required for learning. The agency's profit in this investment will be evident later, when the workers are no longer trainees.

Needless to say, the content of central training sessions should be kept closely related to the workers' practice. One of the best methods of achieving this aim is to have a great deal of class discussion, making it possible for the training staff to find out what the workers are really thinking about, and to determine the problems that concern them in their practice. It is always a temptation for a new group of alert, young, recent college graduates to be academic and loquacious about theories and large ideas when they enter group training sessions and are freed momentarily from their day-to-day jobs. This intellectual interest is, of course, a sign that they are alive and healthy; it is to be valued and encouraged. Yet, as this is a job and not a school experience, the discussants must be led gently to matters which directly involve the practice to which they will be returning immediately.

The attempt to thus structure the training session does not suggest that there is not room or time for skillful teaching of larger ideas, of concepts and principles. It only means that central training sessions must at all times be kept related to the job at hand. The new worker who must examine in depth each new idea, and who has appropriate concern with the meaning behind all new things he hears about, may well be the worker who should be encouraged to go on to graduate school. In view of the fact that it cannot be expected that most of the newly hired social work staff in public welfare agencies will attend graduate schools on a full-time basis, the in-service training program has to be viewed as a self-contained program not directly related to professional education in social work. When in the formal learning situations in the agency's in-service training program some of the new workers appear to be potential graduate students, they surely must be cherished and encouraged from the very beginning, but while they are participants in the agency's training program they cannot be confused with graduate students. As for the others, the bulk of the new staff, it is possible that some among them may be workers in the agency primarily because they did not want to attend graduate school and are seeking through this employment to avoid further study. There is no way to select out one group from the other at this early stage of training, so it becomes a teaching task of no small proportion to determine the exact level of instruction, and to know precisely how far the group is prepared to delve into content. Naturally, groups will vary according to hiring periods, for sometimes recruitment efforts are directed toward different sources of potential workers. The question of striking the right level of learning in a group where there are such variations in motivation, intellect, experience, and background is a very challenging pedagogical problem, one that is never present to the same degree of complexity in a graduate school, where at least the class has in common some degree of motivation to study.

There are several means open to the staff trainer for relating the content to be taught in central training sessions to the tasks the workers will be carrying out in their practice in accordance with their particular abilities. First, the use of an open course plan with flexible objectives will make it easier for the trainer to entertain discussion, to help the workers roam through ideas and ask pertinent— even though sometimes irrelevant—questions. With an ear kept attuned to the learning needs of the group the trainer cannot help but hear the most significant problems encountered in practice. He can then teach, to the limit possible, about those very areas of concern. The plan for the session may dissolve somewhat, but with sufficient experience with several groups of this kind the training staff will be able to develop flexible course plans that can be accommodated to foreseeable responses of the group. This pragmatic approach will never achieve the same heights or depths of knowledge and skill as a more theoretical method applied in an academic setting. It primarily aims to help the workers modify their attitudes and learn to do their jobs better. These are not unreasonable educational goals, nor are they out of context with the reality of the public welfare agency and the ordinary provisions of administration.

A second way in which the central training sessions can be kept closely related to the workaday world of the new employees is for the staff development program to become thoroughly integrated with the practice of the training units. The content level of central training can be raised

only to the degree that the worker's practice is enriched
by appropriate on-the-job training. Suppose, for example,
that in the group sessions the matter of social study was
under consideration. The training staff characteristically
would be eager to teach about the collection and organization of psychosocial data, and the workers would be full
of questions about the process. As long as the supervisors
of the training units were alerted to this interest and were
helped to know how to teach the social study process
through the workers' caseloads, the content of central
training sessions then would be supported and classified
by the workers' practice, and the social study process
could be taught in greater depth. The opportunity to put
into practice the knowledge being taught carries for the
new workers a greater guarantee of optimum learning
conditions than they would have if they were taught theory in the protected isolation of the classroom without
reference to the actual field experience.

The third way in which the content of central training
sessions can be correlated with the workers' practice experiences is somewhat the reverse of the way we have just
described. This form prescribes that the training unit supervisors themselves participate as fully as possible in the
planning and evaluation of the central training sessions, or
even teach a few of them themselves. There are reasons in
favor of this procedure which may not be immediately
obvious. Following such a pattern of participation, the
supervisors would be able to feed into the central training
sessions the ideas and issues that confront the workers in
their daily practice. Simultaneously, the supervisors
would have fairly direct access to what is going on at all
times in the central training sessions. There would be reg-

ular meetings of training staff and supervisors before and after the sessions. The continuous active involvement of the supervisors would be crucial to the relatedness of central training sessions with training unit practice. As complementary aspects of in-service training, the programs would rely upon each other for strengthening.

As far as the organization of central training sessions is concerned, many possible adaptations of the program exist all over the world. They range from having the newly hired staff attend classes for a period of time before they begin on their jobs, to a set number of sessions that go on concurrently with the workers' training unit experience, and finally to sessions that are introduced only after the workers have been on staff for a certain period of time. While the second approach of concurrent training methods would be preferred because of the advantages of dovetailing both kinds of learning experience, there is, of course, no definite rule about when or how long the sessions need to occur to be most effective. The timing, spacing, and duration would undoubtedly have to depend upon the physical traveling distance of the central training sessions from the training unit practice, the nature of the job pressures at the agency which would affect the matter of sparing workers to attend sessions, and the availability of training staff. It is not important that we concern ourselves here with rigid scheduling; we would not, in any case, know what is best for every situation. The essential thing to keep in mind is that a relationship must be provided for the workers between the two kinds of learning, and that where possible both kinds should continue on a dependably regular basis for as long as the newly hired workers are considered by the agency to be trainees.

Now let us look at some aspects of method and content that are involved in central training sessions. It might be helpful in this connection to use two illustrations to examine how content can be taught either appropriately or inappropriately. The choice of these illustrations is based not so much on the significance of their content as it is on the impact of the improved method upon the training group.

The first example concerns a situation in which an administrator in a public welfare agency was invited to talk with the group in central training about certain essential matters concerning residence of clients and their financial resources. In the first session the administrator arrived at the training meeting armed with a supply of forms used by the agency in establishing residence and determining resources. After all, the two tasks may be accomplished best through the use of forms. Usually there are questions to be asked and answers to be given about those two important areas of a family's life. Generally, the answers are matters of fact and require limited judgment or decision-making. Probably the most important thing to teach new staff members in handling these questions is that a good human relationship is required between them and their clients if the answers are to be forthcoming without fear of threat.

Before a formal staff development program existed at the agency in question, the administrator would pass out copies of the forms and go over each point with the group of new workers, always cautioning about accuracy and clarity. While it is not an unreasonable expectation that the staff take care of such matters correctly, the problem we are considering here is how such procedures are best taught so that the staff will indeed carry out their tasks with accuracy. The use of a group meeting for this purpose is probably wasteful of time and effort, and a rote method of teaching about forms may well antagonize the group and close them off from discussion and from hearing important ideas from the leader or from each other. No group can remain attentive to filling out practice forms when those forms are unrelated to real cases that they know. The most that can be expected of group teaching of routine tasks is routine behavior. The only way we know to train for independent and responsible practice is to make the content meaningful and immediately useful. This process can best be achieved by a supervisor, in a training unit, as the new worker discovers the relationship of residence and resource forms to the job he is doing. In this way, in-service training is concentrated on service to the client as well as accountability to the agency, rather than on the accurate filling out of forms in a routine, imitative way.

The next time the administrator was invited to speak to the group about residence and resources, the staff development consultant worked with him beforehand. The consultant had him meet with the training unit supervisors to discuss the issues that were bothering them and their workers in this area, and the things they saw as important for the workers to learn about their jobs. In thinking through the content and the method of teaching it, the administrator recognized that his goal was a larger one than accuracy in filling out forms, and that he had to inject more excitement into the subject so as not to "lose" the group again. He passed out no forms, but began at once to ask the group what they thought of residence and resources, why those areas were important as components of eligibility in the public welfare agency, and, most important, what they didn't like about the policies regarding them. Naturally, the group participated in an exciting discussion of the meaning of eligibility and accountability, and they were helped to understand significant issues and problems without reference to a single form or caution about accuracy in reporting. Thus, the involvement of the workers took precedence over the completion of forms.

This is an example of the way in which even the most technical material may take on color and meaning for a new group of staff obligated to master it. The overriding result of this kind of agency training is that new workers will be less apt to resist such routine tasks, and will be able to integrate their learning and acceptance into their practice more readily the next time they see a client. In this form of training it is not imperative that new workers accept antiquated methods of establishing eligibility. They may in fact protest the entire procedure, but at least they will understand the reasons for its existence. A creative training staff and a secure administration will seize this as an opportunity to enlist the staff, new as they are, in the arduous struggle of public welfare with the community at large to reexamine the concept of a rigid means test. As a group of new workers are taken along with the administration's concerns in such important matters, they will become almost immediately part of the social welfare movement to a degree that would never be possible if they were merely brainwashed into acceptance of an inadmissible idea. A full discussion of the history behind the means test, the forces in the community that insist upon it, and the alternative measures being considered, will in even a single training session draw out the workers' lay attitudes and will entail attendant learning about almost every aspect of their practice.

The second example of different modes of teaching in central training sessions has to do with the teaching of staff in one department—in this instance Child Welfare —about the structure and function of the total agency, particularly the department of Public Assistance. Naturally, the relationship between those two functions of a public welfare agency is, to say the least, intimate, despite the fact that in most public welfare agencies they are separately structured. Again, this illustration contains a before-and-after episode, and again the difference lies in the approach. Prior to the presence of a staff development consultant, a senior staff member from the Public Assistance department was generally invited to instruct a group of newly hired workers about his department's program. Usually this involved drawing a chart of organization on the board, and developing point by point the grand list of functions carried out in Public Assistance. The training group sometimes copied the list dutifully, even though it appeared in greater detail in the office manuals they had at their desks. The brighter members of the group, having looked at the manuals, or having greater awareness of their natural limitations in being able to absorb or retain this kind of information, simply tuned out of the discussion and were lost completely by the group leader.

As in the other instance cited, the staff development consultant met with the representative to discuss his objectives and the appropriate educational methods for carrying them out. Again, the training unit supervisors met to explain to the staff development personnel their views of the most important aspects of public assistance the new staff would need to learn. As a result, the next time the same subject was taught to the new workers in their central training session, the leader did not have to teach everything he knew about public assistance, but rather settled for the more feasible training goal of helping the group to develop constructive attitudes toward the work and staff of his department. He sharpened their interest in asking their supervisors about potential services for their clients and for help in effecting proper referrals. He began his session by identifying those places where the services of the two departments converged; where the group as Child Welfare workers would be particularly involved in the Public Assistance program. He entertained their questions and, what was most important, he encouraged their criticisms so that he could deal with them directly in the session itself. He moved on to some of the reasons for communication difficulties between the two staffs, and he dramatized through case material the way in which Public Assistance budgets were arrived at, and other similar matters.

The result of this approach to teaching about the Public Assistance program—as in the case of the group concerned with determination of eligibility—was not that the group learned very much about policies and procedures, but that they had a greater readiness to know about the program as it was explained later by their supervisors, written about in their manuals, and illuminated by their own clients in their practice. Naturally, their curiosity was awakened and they became more receptive to direct and indirect learning about the program itself, both during and after the single training session. The most important results of this shift in objectives of the training session were a sharpening of interest and a change of attitude toward the serious business of public assistance.

Let us recapitulate the important underlying premises in this approach to central training for newly hired staff. There are some principles for us to recognize in the previous discussion of teaching methods.

In the first place, integrated learning in social work takes place primarily through supervision of practice, where meanings can be derived from real case situations with which the worker is involved. It would be pretentious to assume that the learning in a central training session, no matter how frequent or how well taught, could ever substitute for on-the-job training through supervision.

Secondly, among the varied purposes of central training sessions as they supplement training unit experience, is the primary objective of providing a comfortable arena for the new workers where they may raise questions, learn content that will affect their attitude toward clients and toward further learning, and find a measure of security and identification through associating with each other in an agency-sponsored group.

The third principle of central training is concerned with its relatedness to the ongoing practice of newly hired workers, the involvement of their supervisors, and the feeding back and forth of content from central training to training unit. Thus, the mutual supports that characterize the structure of in-service training for newly hired staff members control the content that is taught. The emphasis placed upon this content may tend to be more pedestrian in its problem-centeredness than some might wish. Yet, the pull toward problems and practice is justified because this kind of learning can be more easily integrated by working staff, and because the kinds of tasks they perform do not always require theoretical development. This should not mean that the trainer in staff development must withhold knowledge from the group or reduce the level of content to the point of boredom. It does mean that he must imaginatively expand the routine material the new staff must learn, taking his cues from them and their training supervisors so as to keep central training sessions closely connected with their practice. It means that the simplest procedure must be taught conceptually, with emphasis on the reasons behind it, so that the workers will be stimulated to think and to question.

There are some difficulties in describing exactly what the total plan of central training sessions should be, because so much is dependent upon the functions to be carried out by a particular group of newly hired social workers. One of the chief differences between the content that is best taught centrally and that taught in training units is that in the larger group, which is temporarily separated from immediate practice, it is more appropriate to teach that general content which relates to every case that a worker might carry in his practice. This serves to introduce or reaffirm in a general training session the specific material being taught under individual supervision. Usually such content can be better taught in a group, and supervisory time devoted to application of this general knowledge to individual cases.

For example, in the central training sessions the new workers may be taught the importance of social study, particularly the observation and collection of facts that help to explain a case situation. In their training unit experience they will focus on the social study of their particular cases, each containing different characteristics, each calling for individualized assessment and organization of data. The principles relating to this process may have been taught in the central training sessions, but they will come to life only as they are specifically applied to the cases which illustrate them concretely.

One of the ways in which the content of central training sessions can be related to the interest and competence level of the new workers is by the involvement of their training unit supervisors in planning from the start. No other group in the agency, including the training staff, will know the nature of their learning needs better. The role of the training staff is played through helping the supervisors understand the content that determines appropriate teaching methods in group training, supervisory instruction, and written material such as agency manuals, instructions regarding procedure, office memoranda, and similar media. The training staff can then work toward development of the supervisors as primary educators in the agency setting.

It would probably be effective and timesaving (not an unimportant consideration in an in-service training program that rests in the administrative structure) for central training sessions to include some of the following broad areas of content:

THE AGENCY: Description of its purposes, functions, structure, and organization, including the supports it derives from the community and the mandates required by legislation.

THE COMMUNITY: Including historical trends in public

welfare, attitudes toward public welfare, and the reasons for accountability as well as for some of the questionable procedures staff is asked to carry out. Here we can include discussion of the range of health and social services available outside the agency.

THE CLIENTELE: Including the kinds of needs all people have in common, and the particular needs of people who are poor and who require the range of public welfare services. This area of content might also include an elementary discussion of the relationship between inner and outer needs and the ways in which people typically defend themselves from problems and anxieties. Such content development would not be complete without emphasis upon the factor of differences among people—physically, culturally, psychologically, and intellectually—which makes it necessary for the worker to recognize and accept these differences in his clients. Finally, weight must be given to the notion that people have varying strengths, evidenced by each individual's capacity to deal with his problems, to function even on a limited basis in a complex society, and to form relationships no matter how unsatisfactory some of these may seem to be.

THE WORKER AND HIS METHOD: Here we are concerned that social workers conduct their practice in a manner that combines objectivity with compassion, intelligence with judgment, and clarity of purpose with responsible action toward the clientele and the agency.

Throughout the central training sessions it is important to weave in content relevant to the workers' attitudes and values. This material is best communicated indirectly as attendant learning, because attitudes and values are not ordinarily changed by direct confrontation. More likely they are modified by demonstration, new knowledge, and meaningful experience. As newly hired workers learn from and observe their supervisors, senior colleagues, administrators, and others on staff to whom they may be exposed, they learn a great deal about social workers' attitudes and values and they draw upon those models of behavior for their own modes of practice and their own sense of commitment.

Suggestions as to the arrangement and timing of areas of content are dependent upon the requirements of the agency and the demands of specific practice. The personnel available to teach the materials will vary in every agency, and to that extent the content will be taught more or less fully, and more or less well. In an in-service training program particular value is usually found in a structure that can be flexibly adapted to changing conditions of learning. The organization of content and method in the manner we have described is easily subjected to modification according to the ability of the training personnel or the newly hired workers and their supervisors. It is adaptable to the demands of agency timetables, office space, and favored practices. In a public welfare agency, unlike a graduate school, the conduct of a training program is conditioned by administrative demands; it is subject to a host of priority decisions, shifts of personnel, and job pressures. A training program that is too rigidly structured will inevitably be seen as an obstacle to the agency's practices, a competing rather than a supporting function. On the other hand, when it is flexible and sensitive to the workaday realities of the agency's life, it will more readily find a significant place in the total agency program.

In this description of training unit and central training

programs we can observe one method of training newly hired workers in a public welfare agency. An important factor in this approach is the maximum amount of participation by higher levels of staff, particularly the training unit supervisors, in the training of workers. This kind of program is less apt to engender isolation of the new worker from the mainstream of the agency's practice. Also, there is a greater tendency for the content to remain job-focused and thus discrete from professional education. A blending of the two kinds of training would not in itself be damaging; but in the light of the effect of agency settings upon educational aims it would be unfeasible as well as unwise to attempt to join the two.

At every turn the program of training just described provides for modifications that might occur because of limitations or opportunities in agency, staff, and program. This concept of a training program provides built-in restraints, a system of checks and balances, that condition the nature of the content so that it may be accommodated to the characteristics of the agency's practices. There will be greater assurance that the newly hired worker will be trained for a particular agency's practices, for working with a specific kind of staff group, and for carrying out those services that are within the scope of the agency. In this kind of project there is no hint of training for other agency programs or for the social work profession. Its sole task—that of readying untrained staff for the work of a public welfare agency—is carried out by means of an integral process with specific job-centered aims.

Chapter Six

In-Service Training of Supervisors
and Experienced Practitioners

In public welfare agencies supervisors are usually promoted to their rank after two or more years of successful
practice as workers. Increasingly, agencies are finding it
possible through local civil service systems to require that
supervisors be qualified through graduate school education of the full two years, or at least one year. In communities where there is a shortage of professionally trained
supervisors, or where most of the incumbent supervisors
have been in their jobs for a long time and seem to be without potential for professional education, there are often,
at this level, parallel promotional lines for professional
and nonprofessional staff. Despite the fairly rapid progress being made throughout the country in staffing supervisory jobs with senior professional social workers, statistical evidence suggests that it will be many years before
this crucial staff group will be characterized as fully
trained professionally. Therefore, we must deal with its
training as we did with the group of newly hired staff, as a
function of the agency's staff development program.

There are several possible groups of supervisors, their

learning needs being less simply defined than those of newly hired staff, who have in common their beginning status and lack of knowledge of the agency. In order to observe the learning needs of the total supervisory staff and decide upon the form of their training, it is important to differentiate among them.

We have mentioned the training unit supervisors whose special function of training new staff brings them into continuous involvement with the staff development program. Another group is that of supervisors who are new to supervision and who are in need of training for that function. (They may also be professionally trained personnel.) A third group are the personnel who carry out new agency programs or who are themselves new to a program.

Finally, there are those supervisors and experienced workers who comprise the largest group in most agencies —the ones who carry out the ongoing program of the agency day to day and year to year. They might not be involved with the training units or with the specialized programs that enrich the agency's services. Often they are not professionally trained, for frequently there are so few trained staff members that when a public welfare agency is able to hire or retain a professional social worker it ordinarily assigns him as a practitioner or supervisor in some special function in the agency, or as a training supervisor. The staff to whom we are referring as the largest group are also the mainstay of many public welfare agencies. They remain at their jobs perhaps because of job security, for without higher education it is doubtful that they would get comparable jobs elsewhere, and if they have been at a particular agency for many years they have money invested in the retirement system. This is the group of personnel that the literature often refers to as "petty bureaucrats" because they have so often grown older on the job, have carried their expertise with them through the long years, and naturally have much at stake in seeing that things continue as they were when they came to the agency. The ways learned in their early years are the ways with which they are presently most comfortable.

It is evident that this large group of incumbent, nonprofessional, middle-aged personnel would not be readily open to learning in a program of staff development. From one standpoint they would have everything to lose, as the introduction of new knowledge and modern methods in practice and supervision would serve to threaten their established ways of working. Even the in-service training of new staff may be a problem to them, for new staff who are young and eager and have been exposed, sometimes before their supervisors, to new methods and content are likely to know more than they do about current approaches. The matter of professional education and its meaning to the old-line supervisors and practitioners warrants particular consideration, because the threat of professionalism has become more real than imagined for them, and the widening gap of knowledge between the staff and the profession is of increasing concern in the wake of the expanded public welfare law.

Some experienced staff will grasp the opportunity to attend graduate school, particularly if it is offered to them with full financial support and educational leave, but there is always a residue who will see no value in any part of professional education. This is surely the hard core group of supervisors, who nevertheless must be exposed to training within the agency in order that the agency may really carry out its new programs of prevention, service, and rehabilitation. There is no justification for not providing training for staff who resist it. An agency-wide staff development program must include this group in its process, perhaps more actively than it does the newly hired young staff.

In addition to the hard core group who will affirm at every turn their disbelief in the values of professional education, there is another group who will take advantage of agency scholarships and will seek to attend graduate school at the first opportunity. Keeping in mind that they may have worked at the agency for possibly twenty years and may never have indicated a previous interest in attending even a part-time course paid for by the agency, it is worth-while to look a little more closely at their present concern with graduate education. For some, it may be that they have seen the handwriting on the wall, and as they are ambitious and wish to be in the running they will, of course, recognize the necessity for attending school. However, for others it would be unfortunate indeed if the graduate schools themselves did not look closely at these applicants. Not unlike Rip Van Winkle they have awakened to a new reality, but it does not necessarily follow that they have been able to accommodate themselves to the changed conditions of their situations.

Even with the current pressure on schools of social work to educate all of the personnel sent to them by public welfare agencies, it may be unwise to deny that some senior people who apply do not wish really to attend, but rather want only to have attended. The schools may look to their programs and their standards if they accept such people only because the agency sends and finances them, and the agencies may look to their programs as well when those senior staff people return to work literally armed with a master's degree in social work. For if their motivation is questionable in the first place, it would not be surprising for them to take up their new jobs as professionals, moderately changed if at all, but protected by their new status.

Finally, among this group of supervisors who comprise the largest number of permanent senior staff in public welfare, there are those who should attend graduate school if the opportunity is offered, because they are intelligent and flexible, because they have gone as far as possible on their own and really want higher education, and because they will be better supervisors as professionals. Many of this number may have missed the opportunity for financial support of their professional education when they were young workers. To the extent that they have the appropriate motivation and potential they should be selected quickly by the agency for the educational leave program. There is probably no greater investment in personnel than for an agency to send a seasoned, experienced supervisor to school for two years, and such a valuable staff member who is also potentially a good graduate student should receive the utmost in support from school and agency in his education.

It may appear to be more complicated to separate out so many groups of supervisors when it would seem simple to consider the total group as a target of in-service training. In the long run, even though it is a bit more burdensome administratively to do so, one must adapt to the differences that are inherent in large staffs so as to gear the content and method of training appropriately. The definition and organization of staff grouping is probably the primary initial task for the consultant who is embarking upon a staff-wide program of in-service training. Always, the question must be asked, "What are we training for?" Then the grouping will more readily fall into place. Furthermore, the training programs within an agency do not have to involve all personnel at one time. In addition, the plan of training and the persons who will do the direct teaching of staff will differ according to the kind of group and the aims of the program.

Every public welfare agency will have its own natural grouping of staff, some that fall naturally into bureaucratic structural lines, others that converge around particular programs, and still others that are defined by length of service, function, and previous training experience. It is always best not to insist upon a rigid plan of organization, so that one can, as the need arises, recognize new approaches to the organization of training groups. Here we can speculate about some groupings which may bear a similarity to many public welfare situations.

In the previous chapter we described a training approach to a natural grouping of public welfare staff—the newly hired practitioners. Pursuing the description of natural staff groupings who are performing functions on mutually comparable levels of employment, we move next to the experienced practitioners, those who are not trainees but who comprise the bulk of staff who have been employed at the agency for a period longer than the training period of weeks, months, or a year. In an urban public welfare agency which employs hundreds or thousands, obviously it would be necessary to create manageable subgroupings of experienced workers, and there are countless ways of arriving at such groupings. Groups may be differentiated according to departments or divisions if they are small enough, or units within divisions. The agency has to be very clear in its rationale for grouping staff, for there is a relationship between the structure and function of in-service training. The staff development program cannot ever assume responsibility for amassing an almost total group of staff of any kind with the immediate aim of "improving their practice." This, of course, is the ultimate aim of staff development for all of staff at all times, but each part of the training program is more readily understood and thus welcomed by the staff as well as the administration when everyone involved in it knows what it is to be about. It may be concerned with implementation of new service amendments, school dropouts, unmarried mothers, referrals to community agencies, or almost any subject that is a concern of the agency and the staff. Thus, when there are no structural arrangements that lend themselves to differential grouping, the subject matter or job interests of the staff can be the determining factors.

A large natural grouping is, of course, the supervisory staff, which has the complex characteristics just described. Often in staff development programs supervisors are dealt with as though they were practitioners; in other words, supervisors are sometimes included in training programs with workers on the assumption that they, too, need to learn about problems of school dropouts, unmarried mothers, etc. This learning need may well exist, and exposure to new knowledge is usually all to the good. However, it is erroneous to treat supervisors as practitioners in a training situation, not because they may not at times need the training, but because they are in actuality supposed to be performing a different function from that of practitioners in the agency.

It is commonplace to hear from public welfare supervisors that the rate of turnover of personnel is so high and the quality of staff so poor that they must do the work themselves. The inevitable result of this kind of practice is that the work does indeed get done more efficiently and better perhaps by the supervisor, but the worker then loses out on the opportunity to be supervised, withdraws from responsibility for his caseload, and finally, because he no longer can see the meaning in his work, leaves the agency, and the circular pattern of staff turnover and supervisory takeover is begun again.

One of the ways to enable staff to carry out those functions which are appropriate to them is to provide practice training for the workers and supervisory training for the supervisors. It is just as possible to teach a group of supervisors about supervising workers who are carrying cases of school dropouts and unmarried mothers as it is to teach them directly about the case, which they will not or should not be carrying anyway.

Then there is the matter of teaching supervision itself which we will examine more closely a little later. Often even experienced public welfare supervisors have had no formal training in the content and method of supervision. When such is the case in a particular public welfare agency, the staff development program will need to pick up on this training task, even though it may seem late in the course of events to introduce this formal content to incumbent supervisors.

Another level of staff which lends itself easily to grouping for training purposes is that of the case supervisory personnel, who have responsibility for the operation of groups of units, which are in turn under the direction of unit supervisors. The case supervisory group of staff are, of course, doubly removed from practice with clients, and their training program should be related more to the tasks they carry out with supervisors of cases than to the actual practice on the cases. This suggests that the content of training for this group would entail one part supervision, one part administration, and one part knowledge of practice itself. It is difficult to generalize about the characteristics of case supervisors in public welfare agencies; so much depends upon their number in a given agency. Where there are only a few on this level, perhaps the training program would operate best in a consultative fashion. Where there are more, perhaps twenty-five or fifty, then a training group would form naturally.

What is the preferred kind of content to be taught this top level of staff in the bureaucratic hierarchy? In accordance with the principles we have set forth about the process of staff development, the most effective aim of the training program with case supervisors would be their involvement in the training of the lower levels of staff for whom they have the chief responsibility. All that we have said about supervisors as civil servants can be doubly stated for case supervisors, who are generally older and more entrenched in their functioning. It would be all to the good to be able to organize a training program with appropriate case supervisory aims and ask this staff to attend for a certain number of sessions. But it would generally be foolhardy to do so without at the same time taking into consideration their natural resistance to exchanging an authoritative for a learning role in the agency.

The higher the level of staff, the more difficult it is to involve them as learners. One way to do so is to engage them in the role of participant as well as learner, and to utilize meetings of case supervisors as "curriculum planning" sessions. This group would know better than any what the learning needs of staff are; they would be closer than the staff development personnel and most administrators to the actual practice life of the agency as a whole. Therefore, they should be consulted regarding the kind of training indicated for lower levels of staff. The fact of their participation will in itself involve them in the outcome of the training program for others, and in this unthreatening situation they will be able to support the staff in their new learning. Inevitably they also will be exposed to new learning under the suggestions of the staff development consultant.

Before leaving the subject of the organization of groups within the agency as targets of the staff development program, a word should be said about the agency administrators. We have commented repeatedly upon the necessity for the continuous involvement of all levels of personnel, for the sake of supporting the training of lower levels of staff as well as for their own learning. Naturally, the higher up one goes on the civil service ladder, the more entrenched one finds the staff to be. Those on the upper echelons are further removed from the need to learn their jobs, and, generally, more resistant to the teaching of new knowledge and skills. Nevertheless, those groups may be the very ones who are in the greatest need of staff development services, and the responsibility to provide such services cannot be abdicated merely because the groups are difficult to work with. Imagine the fruitlessness of an all-out effort to effect in-service training for the practitioners and supervisors in an agency where the administrators are not accepting of the training program or anything it has to contribute in the way of new ideas! This could be said more strongly by suggesting that when there are limitations in time and effort available for training manpower, it is the better part of wisdom to institute a training program for the top level of staff first, working down the scale as opportunities become available. The kind of staff development process we are advocating is based entirely upon staff support, our premise being that without it there is no hope for the long-standing success of training efforts, and there is less expectation that the training program will be reflected in the total practice of the agency.

In the light of this pattern of staff development, it may become clear why experts so often recommend that the consultant in staff development be administratively related to the chief officer or commissioner in the public welfare agency. Only as the training program receives his support, only as he is helped to understand the reasons for the meeting of small groups of staff away from their desks an hour or two at a time, only as he is able to recognize the relevance for his agency of the content being taught, can the staff development program make any headway. This principle holds true all the way down the bureaucratic line.

In view of the requirement of high-level involvement, we can see immediately that the most well-endowed staff development office, complete with professional consultation, library space, offices, meeting rooms, and clerical services, will not be able to fulfill the expectations held out for it if the person in charge does not have direct responsibility and ready access to the chief administrator.

In fact, one would have reason to be wary if a staff development office were provided with all of the essentials but no access to the power system.

Having settled upon some principles for grouping experienced practitioners, supervisors, case supervisors, and administrators, we are ready to consider a variety of approaches to the in-service training of these groups. Again, there is no particular way that is right at all times for all groups, but it is nonetheless useful to explore some interesting methods that might seem appropriate in a particular public welfare agency. Priorities always have to be determined by the agency involved, depending upon the particular learning needs that are pressing. For example, a pending promotional examination for supervisors would naturally require that the staff development consultant subsequently devise a program of training in supervision for the group of personnel who will need to be prepared for their new function. This kind of program might even take precedence over one that is devoted to the new service amendments, if both subjects cannot be handled at once.

We have alluded to the question of who will actually do the teaching of content in the training groups. No matter how renowned the consultant may be he cannot do it all, and even if he were able to it might be well to consider his role as that of trainer of the trainers, who might be selected case supervisors, or even supervisors of workers. Where there are professional staff in the agency it might be sensible to draw them into this service at times.

In keeping with our view of the staff development process, the less disturbance in the balance of personnel within any training group the greater the potential receptivity of the group. As long as it is a fact of bureaucratic life that outsiders are not too well tolerated, then it would seem to make excellent sense to enlist the best possible leader from within the group and help him to teach the necessary content to the others, with the help and guidance of the professional consultant.

Another reason for diluting the teaching strength in a public welfare agency is completely practical—the fact that the training staff available is generally insufficient to meet the needs of a large public welfare staff.

It seems to follow that training needs become increasingly defined throughout the agency once employees recognize the value of the staff development program. The greater the success of the program the greater the demand, and the greater the necessity to develop agency trainers.

A case illustration of the way in which the staff development process we have been describing worked in a large urban welfare center will help to clarify the method. The potentialities found in its use in a complex organization of 175 practitioners in one neighborhood center should have bearing upon its appropriateness as a training method in a small or rural agency. In fact, where the agency is small and must share its training staff with other agencies in a county, there is increased applicability of this case example. The chief characteristic of the training structure to be described is that the supervisory staff itself was called upon to carry out the bulk of direct teaching of practitioners. The training consultant did not abdicate responsibility for the training of staff; on the contrary, the process demanded of her more arduous attention, more activity, and more intense involvement with the staff trainers than direct teaching would have required.

Specifically, the case example concerns the in-service training of 175 nonprofessional social work practitioners in the public assistance department of a public welfare agency. Those workers were to some extent called experienced, in that the greater number of them had completed their training unit process, which had gone on for about a month. The range of their tenure at the agency was from a month to twenty years, with the bulk of the staff being with the agency, although not necessarily in that particular center, for from two to five years. The chief administrator of the center was a professional social worker who called in the staff development consultant because of her deep concern over the uneven level of practice throughout, and the effects upon staff morale of the lack of grasp of the complexities of their caseloads.

The consultant then met with the administrator and her administrative and case supervisory staff, and together they pondered the exact nature of the learning needs of the staff. They were of two kinds—one in the supervisory area and the other among the total worker group. After a few such meetings where everyone had his say and aired his reasons for the situation in which the center found itself, it was decided to develop three kinds of training groups: one for most of the 25 supervisors on matters of supervision; the second for the staff of workers, divided into seven training groups of twenty-five people each; the third composed of seven supervisors from the line, none of them professionally trained except for one who had had one year of social work education some years before. Those supervisors were selected because to the administrative staff they seemed to be stronger than other supervisors, more acceptable to the practitioners, and particularly interested in assuming the task of teaching the seven groups of workers. Otherwise, this little group of potential trainers was not too different from the larger group of supervisors; we might almost say that they were chosen arbitrarily.

The training plan was aimed at involving the entire staff of the center in continuous group training sessions weekly for three months, or for about fifteen sessions. As holidays were to intervene and absences were anticipated, there was also provision for makeup sessions in order to ensure the workers' full participation. The reader who is familiar with the daily work life in a public welfare center will surely appreciate the administrative effort that went into scheduling the training sessions so that they did not all fall at the same time and so that there was always sufficient staff available to man the units during the time the training groups met. A vast program like this could not have been planned, much less carried out, without the complete support and assistance of the chief administrator. The administrative assistant in the center carried full responsibility for scheduling and seeing to it that workers attended sessions or had their makeup time.

While the plan was to enlist the seven selected supervisors as teachers of the groups of workers, the staff development consultant played a major role in working with them weekly to plan their sessions and to evaluate the happenings of the previous sessions. The chief administrator attended these teaching meetings in order to remain involved and to ensure that the content was kept close to the practice needs of the center. The consultant developed teaching material from cases submitted by the workers themselves, as their first cry was that they wanted the training sessions to be about problems which faced them. The next step was to prepare the teaching notes on these cases, for it must be kept in mind that the seven supervisors had never taught large formal groups and had not used case material conceptually with their units. Later on in the program it became an important part of the seven supervisors' sessions for them to work together in developing the teaching notes themselves. At the end of the three months' training program the workers were given a quiz, in which they were tested on the content of their sessions.

Throughout the program the rest of the supervisors met regularly with a member of the staff development program, and they had an opportunity to evaluate continually the effect of the training sessions upon practice. Finally, again by way of evaluating response but also as a "gift" to the hard-working staff, a movie was shown about interviewing and the total group was given the opportunity to talk about the training program.

The efforts put into the program and the positive responses that derived from it, in addition to the fact that the entire plan demonstrated total involvement of the staff, would suggest that its success was a foregone conclusion. To the extent of its fairly modest aims—to raise the practice level, to expose workers to the notions behind the service amendments, to induce them to think about and take a greater interest in their work—the program was indeed a success. Serendipitously, the most dramatic results were to be seen in the seven training supervisors, not only in their improved teaching skills and increased general knowledge, but also in their own attitudes toward clients and workers, which previously had not always been totally constructive. This change in their supervisory behavior was obvious to their case supervisors and the administrative staff.

Beyond those observable gains it is difficult to affirm the

long-range results of the training program, because no evaluative controls were built into it beforehand. Because many of the workers left the center through regular resignations and transfers to other centers, it was not really possible to follow through on the results. If no other effect was felt by the staff and the agency, it was sufficient that the workers liked the program and recognized the validity of the content and the importance of training.

This case illustration of an agency-wide in-service training program illuminates the process of staff development in its observance of two major principles: involvement of the staff, and beginning where the staff is in their knowledge and readiness to learn. It also describes the way in which incumbent staff members can be drawn into the training program even though they may not be expert teachers; the value lies in the fact that they are "of the staff" and that they themselves will learn through the process of teaching. One of the most significant lessons to be drawn from this experience is that where the top administrator shares the aims of the staff development program, training has a greater chance of success. Conversely, if training were to be conducted surreptitiously, its effect upon practice would be seriously mitigated.

Let us now look at other forms of training applicable to public welfare agencies. The one we have just described had to do with the training of practitioners, and while the arrangements were on a mass scale the same process can be observed on a smaller scale by combining one or two units of workers to be taught by a selected supervisor. However, we have said that where a choice must be made to provide training for practitioners or supervisors, it is often best to direct attention to supervisors as the key group. What form can training programs for this group take? Ordinarily they are a smaller and more manageable unit for which to plan, and they generally do not need to be taught the functions of the agency, as they usually will have had at least two years of experience carrying out those functions.

Naturally, if training programs can be planned for supervisors they can be planned as well for the practitioner staff, but we are reminded that the practitioners tend to turn over more quickly; ordinarily they are such a large group it is difficult to provide regular direct training sessions for them. Moreover, as we have said before, there is questionable value in directing a great deal of training effort toward the practitioner group unless and until their supervisors are brought along with the program. The influence of supervisors upon workers is very great indeed, and it is folly to bypass them on our way to direct training of their workers, even if the workers themselves are more amenable to training.

When the administrative decision is made that supervisors should participate in training programs during a specified length of time, workshops conducted within the agency or in conjunction with a local school of social work are effective modes of training for this group. A workshop connotes participation of the group in the development of the content to be studied. Who better than the embattled public welfare supervisor knows the content of his job? The learning that goes beyond mere reiteration of what is already known will depend upon the leader and his ability to enlist the workshop members in moving ahead to areas of knowledge that are unknown, foreign, or alien to them. As there is no way for "vitamin shots" of knowledge to be injected, the group must be enabled to want to learn and to feel no threat from doing so. Here again we can recognize the crucial difference between the agency and the school, the office and the classroom. A supervisor in a public welfare agency will continue to hold his job and carry out his assigned function without necessarily being motivated to learn more than he knows. The student, of course, has to have the minimum of motivation for learning before he even enters a graduate school, and the desire to learn must expand with his ongoing participation in the educational program. This motivation is also a requirement of the in-service training process, but the burden of it lies greatly upon the program, on the degree to which staff development personnel can involve the supervisors so that they will want to learn. It is not suggested here that graduate students are recognizable by their motivation, or that the presence of interest in learning alone differentiates a student from a worker; the difference lies in degree, but also in the specific, conscious commitment of the graduate student who attends a school ostensibly to learn. This may or may not be a goal of the public welfare worker or supervisor, but in any case it is not a requirement of his status.

The composition of membership in the workshops would, of course, depend upon the kinds of supervisors in the agency and the specific learning needs they have. We have alluded to new supervisors, training unit supervisors, those who simply need to be brought up to date about some aspects of the agency's program, and those who require the stimulation of formal group discussion about subject matter that is reflective of their career interests. The workshops can be organized around such clusters of supervisors, and then individual agency decisions will have to be made as to whether or not to place new and old, good and bad, flexible and rigid, professional and nonprofessional staff in the same groups. There are arguments on both sides of the question of homogeneity in groupings; sometimes the advantages of faster development of content in a homogeneous group can be vitiated by the disadvantages of jealousy and hostility on the part of those who are out of the group. Often, a heterogeneous group will generate more stimuli if the teacher is skilled enough to be able to help the members find a common level of interest and a comfortable pace of learning for all.

As in the case of the pattern of training described for practitioners, the training of supervisors can be carried out by case supervisors and administrators rather than by the training staff itself, as long as the training staff takes the responsibility for developing the agency teachers and providing them with appropriate training materials.

The choice of content to be taught to supervisors in public welfare is not easy to decide upon. The aim of the training program is usually the improvement of supervision of workers in one or another area of their practice. Yet, when one actually gets down to the training of supervisors it soon becomes evident that their need for learning is often in the very areas of practice which they are to supervise. This poses a pedagogical problem of some complexity. Does one teach the content itself, or does one teach supervisory method? In social work, as in any field of endeavor where the supervisor must know the job his supervisees are doing, it is impossible to teach methods of working with those supervisees without covering the content of the job first. The difficulty here, as we have mentioned earlier, is that the immediate learning need is usually supervision, and the tendency of many public welfare supervisors is to do the worker's job rather than to supervise him. One way out of this dilemma is to introduce case material and teach it on two levels simultaneously: the case itself, and the practitioner's work on the case. Another way is to set aside a block of time to introduce or review casework content, and then sequentially move into supervisory material. The method selected should depend largely on the knowledge of the supervisors' skills and the inclinations of the training person involved. It is difficult to evaluate one method over the other, but it should be kept in mind that a group of untrained supervisors who have grown up in a public welfare job and have learned their practice through trial and error must first be familiar with casework practice before they can be called upon to supervise that practice. The requirement that both kinds of content—casework and supervision—be included in supervisory training illustrates again the fact that in-service training cannot be rushed beyond the point of staff readiness. In this instance, time is needed to compress two levels of knowledge so that both can be taught meaningfully.

Typically, the content areas to be presented to nonprofessional supervisors in public welfare agencies are concerned with knowledge and skills related to working with the client group. These include material about human behavior, ego-adaptive mechanisms, psychosocial need, the influence of biocultural manifestations upon families, individualizing methods involved in social study, diagnosis and treatment, and rather extensive knowledge about the agency's policies and services and the structure of the community. This content is the bare minimum necessary to give the supervisor as grounding for the supervisory method.

As far as supervision itself is concerned, the first learning task is for the supervisor to organize her ideas about practice into a conceptual form that will enable her to communicate it. Then, there must be understanding of workers and how they differ, the ways in which they learn and resist learning, and the ways they carry into their practice their previous experiences. Finally, the supervisor must be taught how to supervise; how to begin at the worker's level, and to enhance his learning through patient interpretation of his practice experience. She must learn how to enlarge the worker's vision, to build knowledge carefully, to recognize transfer of learning, to allow for learning plateaus, to permit for just enough and no more anxiety to propel the worker to continued learning, and, above all, to permit him to make mistakes in the course of his learning and to achieve a sense of independence as well as responsible accountability.

The extent to which these objectives of educational supervision [1] can be achieved depends largely upon the administrative supports the supervisors can depend upon within the agency. For example, a concomitant aspect of educational supervision is an evaluation of the worker within a prescribed period of time, an evaluation in which the worker participates with the aim of charting his progress in learning. Supervisors must be assured that their educational function is valued in the agency, or neither they nor their workers will be free to assess their practice concerns with any yardstick but quantitative criteria. Only to the degree that supervisors can enable workers to learn

rather than to produce with speed, will public welfare
agencies be able to boast of staff development. Once again
we look toward rational agency procedures to support
staff in achieving educational aims. Without supports
throughout the hierarchy, there can be no expectation of
improved practice despite herculean training efforts.

Inevitably, we are led to the crucial part of any staff
development program in a public welfare agency, that
which has to do with case supervisors and administators,
and ultimately with the validity of the agency's program.
The process we have described for workers and their
supervisors holds true as well for all other levels of staff.
Wherever possible they should participate continuously
in the planning, if not the direct teaching, of supervisors'
workshops and training sessions for workers. By assuming
the role of trainer, case supervisors and administrators will
contribute to the staff development atmosphere of the
entire agency. Their involvement in the training program
will inevitably bring them closer to staff and their problems. They will learn about strengths and limitations in
the agency's practices even as they teach.

Examination of the organization of a staff development
program in a public welfare agency would not be complete without considering two additional groups of staff
who are crucial to the carrying out of services. These
groups lie at the opposite extremes in the line of personnel. One is the clerical and supporting, but nontechnical,
nonprofessional staff; the other, the increasing number of
professional social service staff who are being recruited to
public welfare or are returning from two years of educational leave in schools of social work.

Clerical staff will have mounting significance in public

welfare programs as clerical tasks are reallocated and withdrawn from technical and professional personnel. There is no end of opportunity to include them in the on-going in-service training programs of the workers and supervisors. This group of personnel should be included in social service training because their interest in the outcome of their tasks increases when they relate their duties to client situations. As their jobs are enhanced they will have a greater stake in what they are doing and they will tend to be more efficient. When clerical staff come to the agency without sufficient skills, their training can be devised in a fashion similar to the program described for the social service staff. Office managers and supervisory personnel can well be involved in the decisions about the kind and extent of their training, and can probably do this training themselves, using the consultation services of the training personnel. The same process can be observed for all other types of ancillary personnel in public welfare agencies—homemakers, resource consultants of every type, maintenance crews, etc. The process is certainly viable, and its scope need only be enlarged to include all those people in the agency who are crucial to its functioning.

Finally, there is the group of professional social work staff who often seem like an embarrassment of riches to a public welfare agency that is not yet used to the idea that very soon there will be large numbers of professional social workers in the midst of untrained staff. When it comes to graduates of schools of social work, there is no need for the staff development program to be concerned about teaching basic knowledge and elementary skills. In fact, this group of personnel should be conceived of as being capable of performing quite different functions from the tasks carried out by the untrained workers. There are, nevertheless, important elements of the training program in public welfare that apply to the professional social worker. First, he must be taught the agency's program— its services, policies, procedures, etc. His perception of those elements will differ from that of his nonprofessional colleague, as he will, if he is well educated, place the agency within the total social welfare context, and he will have some strong opinions about its program. He will not have learned those specifics in his graduate training, unless he happened to have had a field work placement in that particular public welfare agency. To the extent that the professionally educated worker needs to learn about the agency, the training task is similar to that directed to untrained staff.

A second aim of in-service training of the new professional worker derives from the notion that he, like a newly hired nonprofessional worker, will need the opportunity to learn about and understand the reality shock he will inevitably experience upon his employment. While the graduate might not be upset about client situations to the same degree as his nonprofessional colleague, he will probably have some kind of reaction to the size of his caseload, the hustle and bustle of the office scene, the expedient measures used to give services to masses of clients, and, not less in importance, the difference in values, attitudes, and practices between the professional and the nonprofessional. The new graduate in particular might need a great deal of help in his responses to the life of the public welfare agency. Even if he is a returning staff member he may need to get reoriented, for if the graduate does not go through a period of careful induction he may express his confusion or resentment in a variety of ways. Graduates have been known to become angry at the agency for not practicing social work well enough, or they may direct this anger toward the school and social work education for not having prepared them for what they call the real world. The professional worker might indeed turn his back upon all that he has learned, or upon the agency that has employed him.

These responses may be channeled at once through a staff development program for professional employees, whereby such workers may be helped to see the agency within the broader social and political context, and their new knowledge and skills as useful and easily adaptable to the public welfare situation. During the next several years the new professional graduates will not have an easy time of it when they become public welfare workers, if indeed the public welfare agencies will be able to attract or retain them at all. Many of the agency programs maintain questionable practices, and in most agencies there are a sufficient number of incumbent, nonprofessional employees to make the going difficult for the professional social worker, who is the personification of the outside threat to the civil service staff.

As we have seen, innumerable important decisions must be made by public welfare agencies in connection with ongoing staff development programs. Always, priorities must be considered and choices made regarding demands upon the workers' and supervisors' time and energy. The formation of training groups sets in motion new structures within the bureaucratic system, and unless those groups are defined rationally and find acceptance among personnel they will prove to be amorphous and their efforts will be self-defeating. The readiness of staff to be trained is often conditioned more by their likes and dislikes than by the objective characteristics of the trainer. The nature of the content to be taught may also predetermine its acceptance and use by staff; if training materials do not derive from the agency's practice they may be viewed by staff as alien and dysfunctional.

This conception of staff development in public welfare as the outgrowth of multiple interweaving forces inevitably directs attention to the forces themselves. Training methods must derive from the total framework of personnel hierarchies, bureaucratic rigidities, and administrative controls. Any other approach to training can only place the staff in a bind where they are pulled by agency restrictions on the one hand and staff development on the other. Success in training cannot be measured by academic criteria, but by integration of new knowledge and skill and application in practice, by retention of staff and improved morale, and by acceptance of the staff development program within the total agency. The degree to which the program remains viable in agency terms generally determines its validity for the total staff.

Chapter Seven

Training Method

The staff development process has been described so far in terms of its structure and content. The third aspect to be considered is the method itself. Strictly speaking, the three components must be integrated throughout, as one cannot be put into operation without the others. In a social agency, where the sole aim of achieving knowledge is its immediate use, the chief validity of the structure, content, and training method in staff development is that when they are appropriately interrelated they serve to enrich the program and practices of the agency. They have been treated separately here only because the process is complicated, and analysis of the parts leads to a more ready comprehension of the whole.

Thus, the method of training has justification only when seen in the total context of staff development. Training methods are fruitless without careful structuring, organization, and participation of staff groups, and proper selection of relevant content. Without consideration of these vital aspects of training, the method might be misconstrued to be identical with the educational methods utilized in schools of social work. The reader who has come along this far through our exposition of the process of staff development in a public welfare agency will recognize that it is the direct relationship of this method to the staff, the agency, and community facilities that distinguishes it as in-service training.

Up to this point we have examined the administrative aspects of staff development—those significant supports and controls that govern the process. Now we are ready to deal with the strictly educational components. They share equally in the process, since it is both administrative and educative in its approach. In this chapter it is not intended that we introduce or review the major theories of learning or modern approaches to teaching. The bibliography contains some general references to numerous current theories. Rather, the training method to be discussed is drawn from many theories and applied specifically to the situation at hand: the training of nonprofessional technical staff in public welfare agencies.

The definitions of education and training will help to orient us in our discussion of method, for recognition of the difference between the two will be clarifying, and ultimately will affect the specific mode of agency training. The dictionary defines education as "the totality of the information and qualities acquired through instruction and training, which further the development of an individual physically, mentally, and morally." [1] In differentiating education from training, the dictionary states further that while "education is the general and formal word for schooling of whatever sort, especially as gained in an institution of learning, training suggests exercise or practice to gain skill, endurance, or facility." [2] Thus, education connotes an open-ended objective, best achieved through a process of unfolding, of developing the thinking processes. On the other hand, training is concerned with adapting to the needs of the situation. Clearly, therefore, a specific aim is involved in the training process which is not inherent in the educative process.

In a practical sense, where in-service training occurs in a public welfare agency there is limited time and opportunity for that luxurious method that will nourish the worker and help him ultimately to find his way in the world of his work. Quite to the contrary, the pressure is always there for him to be trained quickly for the specific job he must do. The matter becomes more difficult in application, for it is often said that training must be effected in an educative manner. The failures that are found in in-service training programs may often be due to excesses in emphasis in either direction. By failures we mean not that the programs are decimated, but that they are merely tolerated in an agency by administration and staff alike, and do not actually achieve the larger aims they lay claim to. Either they indoctrinate without observing the elementals of the educational process, or they educate supposedly for the field or the profession and do not remain closely connected with the job to be done in the agency. One way to strike the appropriate balance is, of course, to observe the process of staff development, beginning where the staff are and involving them all in a program which is administratively supported. Another way to ensure that training is effective is to develop teaching methods that get at the heart of the matter, that reach the staff and enable them to learn.

Other definitions of training will help to set the scene for our discussion of methods and techniques; they will help to ensure that we neither limit inquiry out of our commitment to get the job done, nor permit an aimless pursuit of knowledge in our efforts to produce an educational atmosphere. A definition by Herbert Simon places in-service training squarely where it belongs in the administrative arena:

Training prepares the organization member to reach satisfactory decisions for himself, without the need for the constant exercise of authority or advice as means of control over the subordinate's decisions. . . . Training may supply the trainee with the facts necessary in dealing with those decisions, it may provide him with a frame of reference for his thinking, it may teach him "approved" solutions, or it may indoctrinate him with the values in terms of which his decisions are to be made.[3]

In this statement we can recognize the aims and outlines of content of a proper in-service training program. Obviously, the more complex the agency is in organization of personnel and multifunctions, the greater the necessity to train the staff because, among many other reasons, administrative and supervisory personnel cannot directly oversee the workers' practice at all times. In other words, training is a concomitant of bureaucratic structure, not different except in complexity from the training of apprentices in their crafts. Training is indeed a way of affecting workers' decisions, and the necessity to make decisions characterizes modern public welfare practice.

Within this broad definition of training, which is our frame of reference for all that we shall say about method, we can now turn to the method itself, which is educational in a narrow sense; that is, not in aim as much as in technique. Gilbert Highet, a master of the art of teaching, has described education as:

. . . the art of drawing out what is already within the pupil's mind. It helps the pupil to become what, potentially, he already is. Therefore, when the work is over, the pupil feels that nothing has been given to him, merely that he himself has grown. We know, we who have taught him, but if we are wise we shall never tell him the truth.[4]

Does this statement mean, in a public welfare agency where there is so much in the way of concrete information for the worker to learn, that we do not teach him, but merely "lead him to it" and hope that he will make the content his? The reactions of the administrator, and perhaps even the department of the budget that has created the salary lines for in-service training staff—to say nothing of the incessant demands from the responsible staff and the clientele—all converge upon us when we ponder such an amiable definition of the educational method. We might conclude that this method is more applicable to the grade school or even the professional school, where everyone has time and the pressures to produce are not as immediate as they are within an agency, particularly a public welfare agency.

It may be more to the point in this context to recall that education is not just imparting knowledge, but the cultivation of the ability to think effectively, to communicate, to make relevant judgments, to discriminate among values. To the extent that the individual is freed from the confinements of his previous experience to recognize new and exciting ideas and is enabled to learn how to use those new ideas, then he has gained an educational experience which he can put to use. The key to training for agency or even professional practice is its usefulness. As much (or as little) as is known theoretically about the way in which individuals learn and integrate their learning so they can use it, there is a consensus that they must first somehow be willing and able to expose themselves to something new. Knowledge is seldom a matter of direct disclosure; it is made meaningful in accordance with the cues in one's life experience. As experiences are enriched, so new knowledge becomes meaningful. As workers are taught to think, to examine evidence, and to deal with alternative courses of action, then the knowledge to which they have been exposed becomes useful to them.

These educational concepts and principles are reflected in in-service training. When the newly hired social worker is introduced to the functions of the agency, we do not conceive of his training as a value-laden program primarily, but in a very large sense it is, despite the presence of reams of policies and procedures. Even though the law protects the client and defines in exact detail his eligibility for services, judgments are called for. In applying the means test, decisions must continually be made about needs. If workers could be given prefabricated answers in in-service training they would not be needed, for machines could do the job. The very fact that alternatives are part of the eligibility process suggests that values that are the result of knowledge and experience are deeply involved in its application. In-service training, therefore, is weighted heavily in favor of encouraging the new worker to enlarge his perspective and to look for meaning in his work with clients. Indeed he must do so. Making this point, Wayne Vasey has said, "It may be argued with some justification that organizational behavior is the real determinant of the nature and quality of administration of the [welfare] program, and the law is what people say it is." [5]

A further reason for the need to cultivate the workers' thinking ability has to do with the nature of the clientele. To a large degree, due to the nature of the present public welfare program, the client group contains residual characteristics that are always problematic. Much has been written about the mounting complexity of maladjustment of the welfare clientele, as poverty creates impoverished relationships, social dysfunctioning in all areas of life, and a marked deficiency in well-being. It is now evident that public welfare clients are not merely in need of money. If eligibility for financial assistance were the sole issue, then, as we have pointed out, paper and pencil or a machine could readily determine the answers. The fact that socioeconomic and psychological problems are intertwined in the affairs of public assistance and child welfare clients unquestionably requires skilled personnel to work with such clients, at least in areas of their lives that are beyond the concerns of eligibility requirements. As long as this is necessary, and in the urban, overindustrialized world of today it undoubtedly will continue to be so, social workers will be guided by values—their own, their profession's, the agency's, the community's, and the clients'. It is the self-disciplined control over these values that the educational method is so well suited to provide.

A teacher who functions in a school or an agency must sooner or later become familiar with theories of education. He must at the least be familiar with prevalent assumptions about how individuals learn and thus how they may best be taught. In commenting upon the inevitability of theory, Shoben says:

Whether articulate or covert, processes may be carried out systematically or without regard to any comprehensively formulated cognitive structure; they may reflect a commitment to a particular theory or a willingness to borrow whatever ideas that may be useful at the time; they may be executed intuitively or on the basis of highly objective considerations.[6]

No matter what basis of teaching one chooses, whether it is a well-drawn theory or a feeling about a set of experiences, certain ordering principles must always accompany the process. Content must be classified and priorities decided upon, for every piece of content is not of equal importance. Without some organization of ideas, some conceptual arrangement that will align and relate masses of information, the learner will only hear chaos and will himself be unable to understand the meaning or applicability of the content. Theories, or generalizations derived from a series of events, operate at different levels of explicitness and validity, and in teaching it is not always necessary or indeed possible that theories be ironbound, as in the natural sciences. Let us rather call them working ideas or assumptions, so that we can at least begin; there is always time for modifications based upon experience.

Among the major theories of learning with which the reader may wish to familiarize himself are two that represent the polarity in thinking by educational theorists and psychologists. On the one hand there are theories about reinforcement of learning that are concerned with stimulus and response, drive reduction, and motivation.[7, 8] On the other hand there are theories concerned with contiguity of experience as the basic condition necessary for learning.[9] This latter point of view, derived from Gestalt theory and characterized by associations and "cognitive maps," has reached new heights of popularity through the work of Piaget and his studies of cognitive development.[10] In the social work professional literature, contributions to theories of learning social work have been made by Reynolds,[11] Towle,[12] Hamilton,[13] and Robinson,[14] for example.

Since John Dewey[15] teachers have recognized at least one factor that all the varied theories of learning have in common: that education is more than the acquisition of knowledge, although that is vital to the process; it is, rather, the development of the individual's capacity to reflect on knowledge. As Dewey has said, the aim of education is to produce the informed and logically trained adult —the individual who has mastered the techniques of disciplined thought that will help him to deal intelligently with changing knowledge. In relating this significant aim to in-service training of staff in a public welfare agency, our objective, then, would be to train the worker to think rather than to know. We would train him to examine sources of evidence for his evaluations of problems, not to memorize problems or solutions in themselves. We would train him to wonder about the significance of facts and their inter-relationships, not about the ever-changing facts themselves. We would train him to observe, to listen, to draw inferences that are possible within his limitations of knowledge and experience, and to make judgments based upon his accumulation of evidence. We would train him to be accountable, so that in his technical capacity he will turn to others who are more knowledgeable for help. We would train him to accept individual differences and to control his own biases, and to keep his mind open. Such objectives may be accomplished in an agency through a variety of teaching and administrative means, through the wording of procedures, through supervision, and through group teaching. More concisely stated, the chief aim of in-service training is to effect behavioral and attitudinal changes in the worker as he is taught to think with increasing precision as well as to perform with increasing competence.

The question may perhaps still be asked, "Where and when does the worker learn about public welfare?" The reader may not be satisfied that attitude changes are not a luxury when the worker has yet to learn how to interview a client. The administrator may scoff that thinking is all to the good, but what of the worker's grasp of policy? Even the professional might wonder when, in this scheme, the worker is going to learn about people and methods of helping. The answer to all these concerns is that the worker will learn content that is taught and is available in agency materials, if he is helped to think purposively and to integrate his knowledge, and particularly when his role models demonstrate their own grasp of practice.

Pursuing the question of teaching about people and their behavior, we know that if what is taught is conceptualized and made explicit through drawing of principles, there is a good likelihood that the worker can generalize to other contexts. For example, we would teach a worker that cultural factors affect the way in which parents treat their children, and that this knowledge should affect judgments about parental behavior. Thus, when the worker notices that a parent never visits his child's school, punishes him physically, overindulges him, or wants to send him away to placement, the worker will recall that cultural factors might play a role in such instances. It would be folly to attempt to teach about each potential experience that parents might have with their children. If explicit connections have been made between the worker's observations about parent-child relationships in a case or group of cases, and knowledge about cultural factors, his practice will take on meaning so that the next similar experience he has will bear evidence of the carryover. Obviously, before the worker is able to understand and know about cultural differences, he will have to be freed from his own monolithic prejudices, and, above all else, he will have to care about what is happening to the family. Thus do we observe the coming together of knowledge and attitude.

Similarly, in the matter of interviewing, knowledge of a technique rests firmly in broader content about the way people behave and the role played in relationships by the worker himself. The manner of interviewing is a reflection of the worker's comfort with the nature of his job and what he has set out to learn or do in the interview. It is also an outgrowth of his opinions about his clients, his beliefs about people in general, and his attitudes toward them. Teaching interviewing is not, then, purely a substantive matter.

Finally, in our appeal to the harassed administrator we must consider the worker as a carrier of program and policy. Workers in public welfare agencies always use a certain amount of discretion about their interpretation of policy. Policy may be interpreted rigidly or flexibly, and, of course, it can also be overlooked or ostensibly not known. Surely, the attitudes of workers toward their jobs and the agency in which they work have more than a little to do with the way in which they carry out policy. At any rate, policies are best learned through reading about them in agency manuals, and unless training is conceived of as remedial reading the only direction it can profitably take in the matter of policy indoctrination is to free the worker from his resistance to policy, permit his discussion about its pros and cons, and encourage his sense of accountability.

The insistence upon rapid training of staff, upon teaching the "whole book," and upon the rote memorization of content, cannot but compete with training objectives that are more concerned with effecting attitude changes. To some extent those apparently conflicting aims are adjusted in the course of time, when many kinds of knowledge are brought together in the worker's practice. Also, a clear ordering of content and of the different ways in which it is taught will help to establish the bench marks giving evidence that what the workers are learning is significant and will enrich the program of the agency.

There is a formula for vocational education that is considered classic.[16] One may find it aptly utilized in army manuals, in publications of police and fire academies, and often in the training materials of personnel offices in a variety of bureaucratic programs. In that formula the process of training moves from explanation to demonstration, to execution under supervision, to execution without supervision, to testing of results. This is a tidy scheme whereby the teacher can go easily from the simple to the complex and literally train, but not educate, personnel for manual or verbal skills. The key word here is "skills," which characterize most vocations, but not necessarily social work in public welfare. In that area the exercise of skills simply does not exist outside of a context where values and complex knowledge intervene. To the extent that the worker is asked to make decisions and exercise judgment in carrying out his many functions, he must be taught more than craftsmanship.

As for the teaching of skills, we can call to mind a child learning to roller skate, a student typist, and an apprentice television repairman. All of those individuals have in common the requirement that they learn close to exact ways of performing their significant skills. The truth is that within narrow limits there are exact ways to be learned, and thus be taught. This is never so when the subject matter has to do with working with people in any capacity. Yes, we can train a receptionist in an office to answer certain questions and to relate woodenly and without feeling to customers or clientele. But training devoted to skills alone would not help her to discriminate among people and their requests, nor would it prepare her for the day when a question would be asked to which she had not been taught the answer. Moreover, no amount of training in skills would result in her being pleasant to clients unless by happenstance she was so by nature. The public welfare job presently contains so many variables that except for memorization of policies there are hardly any unilateral tasks that can be "trained into" the staff.

In determining method—the how and when of training staff members for the multiple tasks inherent in their jobs —we can utilize several guiding principles.

The overriding notion is that the level of content determines how and under what circumstances it shall be taught. In public welfare the components of practice may be classified as follows:

SUBSTANTIVE KNOWLEDGE: Data on the nature of the job, the agency, the clientele, the community, the program, and whatever content is relevant to a particular setting.

POLICIES AND PROCEDURES: The formulas defining ways in which the program is to be carried out. The greater clarity policies and procedures have, the less need to teach them directly, and the less the worker will suffer from confusion and the client from poor service.

METHOD: The ways in which the services of the agency are carried out, as prescribed by the policies and procedures, and as anchored in the relevant substantive knowledge.

VALUES: The set of beliefs expressed in attitudes and behavior, which govern the worker's total practice. Values are those qualities that make one mode of behavior or another particularly useful to a worker.

These major components of the job, and naturally of the staff development program, are intertwined and connected with each other at all times. We are dealing with them separately here so as to be able to assess where each is best taught in the training program. Emphasis will fall upon one or another factor, but all of the other factors, though quiescent, will be operating together to create a knowledgeable practitioner.

Another way of perceiving these separate but integrated components of the job training program is to differentiate between *primary* and *attendant* learnings. (A third kind of learning, one that is more appropriate to the professional education of the social worker than to the agency-trained worker, is associate learning, which is comprised of all of the content that is peripheral to the primary material—all that may be drawn in to elucidate and broaden the horizon of the learner.)

Primary learnings are those which have to do with the processes and tools that characterize the job. These may include substantive knowledge, policies and procedures, and methods.

Attendant learnings are those which have to do with

values and attitudes, the explicit and implicit system of ideas that determines all of practice. Primary learnings are best taught directly, while attendant learnings are "not taught but caught." They derive from those experiences of the worker that are meaningful to him, and are the result of the coming together of his personal philosophy and his trained agency practice. To an extent one may teach directly *about* values, that is, the knowledge base or the ethical system within which the appropriate values arise. However, the value itself will spring only from the worker's commitment to the system and his conviction that it is right for him. The proverb, "You can lead a horse to water . . ." describes the process best. Values and other attendant learnings are often communicated by the attitudes of the teacher or supervisor, and a worker may change his ideas as he is helped to see validity in new ideas in his practice and relationships. Attendant learning always grows best out of learning to do something.

We have said that the kind of content to be taught determines how and where it shall be taught. Beginning with *substantive knowledge,* clearly this is best taught in groups through the lecture-discussion method. Since substantive knowledge is objective and not affected itself by differences among workers, time and effort can be saved by bringing together groups of staff with comparable backgrounds and interests. There is much to be gained in having a large enough group so that discussion will be varied and fruitful. The determination of size of such a group, where substantive knowledge is being taught, depends somewhat upon the available staff. There are factors in favor of a larger group for beginners and a smaller group for advanced staff. Since the subject matter will be new to new staff they will have less discussion in depth than will experienced staff, and thus more people can be included in the sessions. On the other hand, supervisors' workshops should have a small enough membership to provide for the introduction of content from the supervisors' own experiences. Here, we are not referring to policies, procedures, methods, or values as subject matter, but only to substantive knowledge. Neither are we suggesting that substantive knowledge is not taught in other places outside of formal training session groups.

As for *policies and procedures,* we have hinted previously that there is but one sensible way to expose the staff to these matters, and that is through the written manual or file of written procedures. It may be necessary to provide time for workers to read this material, and to allow for discussion of it in group sessions when it reflects the content being taught or in supervisory conferences when it is closely related to the case under discussion. Apart from this use of the training program to help staff to integrate established agency policies, it is difficult to reconcile further emphasis on procedures with an in-service training program. We must not forget that the administration of a public welfare agency has access to staff through meetings of one kind and another, and usually policies are introduced and discussed in terms of their validity at those meetings. Not all that is done in groups in an agency comes under the heading of staff development.

Method is best taught in conjunction with the worker's practice experience, either in group sessions or in supervisory conferences. Whereas knowledge is taught primarily through lecture and discussion, and policies and procedures through reading, method is taught primarily through discussion of practice. Books, articles, case material, and lectures may be used supplementarily. The easiest way to know how far the worker has gone in his grasp of method and to recognize his blockings and falterings is to have him talk about his conception of what is being considered—but the reckoning will occur only as the worker understands the method, integrates it, and uses it. While there is validity to the teaching of method in group training sessions, its most productive location is the unit where the worker or supervisor practices. Whether the teaching of method in an agency takes place with individual workers or in small units, the process is tutorial. As Socrates taught by asking questions of his students, so the worker will learn best by having his ideas enlarged as he expresses them.

We have indicated the ways in which *values* are most appropriately taught. They appear in every place where other learning occurs; they are taught in connection with substantive content, policies and procedures, and method. They are demonstrated for the worker each time he observes the atmosphere of the intake desk where clients are received, whenever higher levels of administrative personnel come down to where he works, and through the respect he is afforded in office space, a decent salary, and pleasant working conditions. It is useless for a staff development program to emphasize to workers that the public welfare agency "believes in people," unless the agency makes this value evident in all aspects of its program and personnel policies.

Having outlined the areas in which different kinds of content can be taught in a public welfare agency, we can expand our discussion of the educational method itself.

Structure, function, and goals are essential to the process, but in a real sense method is all. There are ordering principles that help to anchor crucial aspects of teaching method, and there are of course techniques themselves. First, let us address ourselves to some of the principles which reflect the specific goals of agency training.

We have implied that in-service training is modeled on the practical, rather than the theoretical, approach. While both pragmatic and theoretical methods of teaching occur in both school and agency setting, there is a difference in emphasis which reflects the difference in educational aims.

In the public welfare agency setting, where the educational job to be done is more or less clearly defined, the pragmatic method can be applied because alternative courses of action are fairly limited. The worker in training has little opportunity to wander intellectually, and he receives a modicum of encouragement to explore conclusions and to pursue the outer boundaries of knowledge. In truth, he is there to learn to do his job better, and to achieve vocational objectives.

The theoretical method is based upon logical reasoning, upon applying general principles to specific instances and thereby drawing conclusions. In the professional school, where the aim is to educate self-directing social workers with strong habits of reasoning, this method of teaching is indispensable for the desired outcome. In the use of the theoretical method in social work teaching, however—to state it in the extreme—it is assumed that there are no "right" answers for the students to learn, but rather that they must continually seek approaches from which they will derive answers that may have many variations. That, after all, is the primary purpose of education —to teach students to think logically, to find interrelationships among relevant facts, and to draw well based conclusions which will guide their actions. In the agency, where action is primary and the diagnostic process not available in the same breadth and depth to untrained staff as it is to graduate students, the theoretical method does not always enhance the purpose of in-service training, which is to enable the worker to practice efficiently. We are not attempting here to evaluate one method against the other, but to show how the two approaches apply to the difference in aim between agency and school programs. The choice of method derives from the established goals.

This differentiation in aims has a vital effect upon the total educational approach of an in-service training program, and consistent clarification is necessary in order to be certain that the agency training program does not turn into an ineffectual program of professional education. A watered down version of the program would only vitiate the effects of training and would negate the purposes of professional education. The differences are reflected in the content presented to workers in training, in the approach used in teaching them, and in the desired aims of the agency training program. A practical postscript can be added to these cautions: A sound administration in a public welfare agency would have second thoughts about supporting a small school within its walls, and the remaining staff in its unreadiness would hardly receive such a program with kindness. The single aim of improved practice within the agency would hardly be advanced.

Beyond this differentiation between practical and theoretical approaches, other choices can be made within the framework of teaching in a public welfare agency. It is not only a question of what is taught, or how the teaching is conducted, but what the context is within which the unit of teaching is to take place—and the purpose. The context, of course, guides the selection of modes of teaching; it is the framework that conditions the content and its development.

Teachers and trainers are not unfamiliar with academic questions relating to whether or not emphasis is placed upon theory or practice, knowledge or skill, principles or problems, and generalizations or specifics. In this same vein we experiment with the educational sequence and usually move from the known to the unknown, the present to the past, and the simple to the complex. In some measure the selection of mode or sequence depends largely on the content to be taught, but on the other hand the choice must be guided by the kind of people in the group and the aims that are held for their learning.

In the agency setting, where theory is not taught to any extent because the agency is not equipped as is a school and cannot support a total educational program, emphasis is best placed upon practice skills, problems, and specifics. In order to teach theory it is necessary to provide concomitant reading time and library facilities, as well as planned intervals of time for lectures and for the students' absorption of the content. Moreover, a field of theory is in itself hardly ever self-contained and limited in its boundaries; it always rests upon other learning and experience and is fed by academic inquiry. The provision of related materials and supporting classroom facilities is precisely the function of the university, and is not in any way the function of the agency. The training staff will undoubtedly teach out of their comprehension of theory, but in an agency setting the emphasis must be placed on its application. That is, the place for theory is in the mind and experience of the trainer, out of which he draws inferences and presents illustrations for the workers.

To help clarify this difficult notion, let us take the example of the teaching of diagnosis to the graduate student in a school of social work. The process is not merely one of figuring out what the case problem is. In order to teach diagnosis thoroughly one must teach as well about human behavior in a psychosocial context, about casework as a total process which includes social study and the collection of data or evidence toward the sequential aims of drawing inferences and deciding upon a treatment plan. Theories about people, problems, society, culture, and method itself are interrelated, and are essential for the social worker's grasp of what the matter is in a particular case situation. We perceive life in ways in which we are conditioned, from a vantage point of knowledge and experience; for the purposes of diagnosis, perception cannot remain merely pragmatic and subject to individual whim or careless definition. Thus, supporting knowledge must accompany the teaching of the diagnostic process.

All this cannot be provided for workers in an in-service training program in a public welfare agency. It simply requires too much else by way of theory, to say nothing of protection in practice while the student is attempting to apply his knowledge of diagnosis.

The fact that public welfare staff is not enjoined from carrying the total casework function has meant that no differentiation traditionally has been made between the diagnostic process and what Finestone has called generalization. An analogy can be drawn to the medical field, where it would be unthinkable to have a medical aide or technician make a medical diagnosis by plan through an organized in-service training program, simply because there was no doctor available. It would be more usual for the technician to confine his judgments to the perimeters of his own competence, and to perform less than a total medical service rather than execute a fallacious one. The dangers in making a misdiagnosis in the field of social welfare may not be as physically dangerous as in medicine, but the effects are never salutary.

In the agency-training situation, the trainer may confine his content to description of client behavior, significant psychosocial symptomatology, expected responses, and typical situations. His emphasis is not upon diagnosis in its accurate sense, but rather on selected facts and relevant generalization. It would seem that the most feasible task that can be carried out by the untrained social worker in public welfare is the gathering and organization of data about the case toward a limited determination of the kind of classification into which that case may fall. This is not a diagnostic process, but a descriptive one. The worker may be trained to see and to hear, to exercise judgment about what seems relevant and significant, and to make some decisions based upon his findings. He may be trained to think about what he is doing, to be accepting of his clients and to be helpful, but always within the limited context of prediagnosis and generalization.

This conception of the public welfare worker's training is consistent with the inductive method of going from simple ideas to more complex ones, from familiar problems to the less familiar, and from present concerns to prior roots. Under this concept training will be concerned with the job the worker is doing, and not with the total field of social welfare, or even with an extended rationale for his actions. He will be given what is possible within the limits of agency training, and he will know that well. He will be trained to his capacity as technician and will not be offered unreal and frustrating aims of competence in areas of knowledge to which he cannot be properly exposed. His training will be geared to his actual situation, which has been likened to that of a man lost in the woods, who is not interested in geography: all he wants is to find his way out.[17]

Having constructed the framework for in-service training, we can now turn to some useful techniques of teaching that are applicable to this process as it takes place within the public welfare agency.

There are two primary forms of in-service training which are modeled after the professional school pattern. They are classroom or central training sessions, and field work or unit practice training. We have alluded to other ways in which the training of public welfare staff can be approached, such as staff meetings and attendance at part-time courses in local schools of social work, but at this time we will address ourselves only to the training session and practice training that occur intramurally as part of the public welfare agency's staff development program.

Training sessions and practice training promote different kinds of learning, and the emphasis given to one or the other in a staff development program will depend somewhat on what the aims of training are in the agency. The training session, utilizing lecture and discussion methods, is generally structured to promote the workers' intellectual grasp of content, while practice training promotes the ability to use and integrate this learning. The distinction between the two methods does not mean that in the training session one does not discuss case materials and in the practice situation one does not teach ideas as well as skills.

Another distinction lies in the focus and organization of training materials. In the training session content is developed around the subject matter, related of course to the level of experience and background of the group members, but nevertheless organized in such a way that the content itself determines the depth, sequence, and timing of presentation. In the practice situation the focus is primarily on the worker as a learner; therefore sequence, tempo, focus, and emphasis are oriented to him in the light of his individual educational demands. It is in the practice situation that lags in knowledge can be readily picked up, and where skills in application can be taught through the educational use of the worker's actual experiences. Since the central training session is structured away from practice, there is inherent in it the element of postponement so that workers can discuss the full implications of the subject matter, whereas in the practice situation the demands for action are immediate, complicated always by the presence of real clients with real needs requiring service from the agency through the worker, even though he is in training.

A further distinction between the two forms of training reflects the vital factor of the client. In a central training session where case material is used for teaching purposes to elucidate a principle or a problem, this material is generally either a finished case, a standardized one, or at least one that is developed for particular teaching purposes. There, through hindsight, the training group may be led to ponder the whole case or a part of it, to wonder why certain actions were taken and what happened as a result. Comparisons may be drawn and generalizations made, but always the emphasis is upon the subject matter being taught, in keeping with the level and pace of the group. In training sessions cases are selected and grouped according to a predetermined teaching plan, to supplement and illustrate ideas.

On the other hand, in the practice situation there is a live client, a case in the making which must be taught as it goes along, before the results of the actions taken are known. Obviously, the responsibility of the worker for his own case is quite different from that of the group in the training session. The unfolding of an actual case is dependent upon what the worker does with his client; it is then not a finished case and its conclusion cannot be totally anticipated. While the teaching from case material differs in the two kinds of training, it should be noted that generalizations and comparisons may be taught in the practice situation as well as in the training session. The difference is not just a matter of "brains and brawn," but rather of emphasis, focus, and timing. In the practice situation those elements depend more on the needs of the client in the case and the worker as a learner. In the central training session, case study is based more upon deductive, back-to-front reasoning, requiring that the worker move from the solution to the problem. In the practice situation, as the case unfolds the worker learns inductively

from specific cases, accumulating knowledge of principles that can be applied to other cases. The aim of the
practice training situation is to teach skills along with
knowledge, in a way that challenges but does not exceed
the worker's capacity, for he must be free to carry out his
job simultaneously with his learning. This achievement of
translating knowledge into practice can best be furthered
by the worker's immediate supervisor, as he helps to ana-
lyze and evaluate the worker's experiences so as to give
meaning to them, toward the aim of building within the
worker a sense of conscious control of his actions.

In the central training session the matter of case selection is not isolated from the total process of staff development. Soliciting teaching cases from senior staff members
or others directly or indirectly involved in the worker's
practice is one of the easiest ways for a training staff to
involve the total personnel of the agency in the program.
Cases may be submitted that illustrate a typical case
problem in the agency, such as unemployment or school
dropout, or they may reflect particular concerns in practice such as recording, policies, workers' attitudes, or interviewing techniques. Once the cases have been collected by training staff they must be assessed for their
useful teaching points and edited sufficiently so that they
are readable and demonstrable. A good case for teaching
may not be the most satisfactory case from a practice
standpoint, but it will demonstrate an idea positively or
negatively. Often a trainer is tempted to use formal teaching cases such as are used in schools of social work, since
these cases have been selected and processed for the
teaching of identifiable ideas. However, the more one bor-
rows from outside the agency for teaching materials, the

less one is able to involve the total staff in the training program. Moreover, in an in-service training situation the practice of using extra-agency cases is as fraught with danger as is the use of extra-agency personnel to give training sessions. Resistance tends to mount in a closed bureaucratic organization when outside elements intrude, whether they are people or cases.

The use of agency case material is particularly well suited to central training sessions, because cases can easily be the springboard for group discussion. Case teaching involves the worker-learner because he can speculate where answers are not absolute, and he does not have to depend upon the erudition of the training person. When the training staff itself is called upon to do the direct teaching in training sessions they will, of course, need to prepare fully and annotate the teaching points in the cases. When senior staff members are drawn in to do this teaching, it is often helpful for the training staff to prepare as fully as possible the teaching points and thematic threads in the case, with the aim that a reasonably well endowed case supervisor will be able to teach from the case.

Before leaving this subject of teaching materials, a word should be said about other kinds of teaching techniques, such as the visual and aural aids which seem to be coming into popularity. In our view movies, posters, charts, as well as tape recordings, have a limited place in in-service training, for if there is an identifiable theme in this book it is that of the need for intellectual and emotional involvement of the staff, so that the participants may learn and their superiors who are nonparticipants may cooperate in their learning. As far as visual aids are concerned, it is never enough to assume that because a subject has been demonstrated or shown in colorful ways it has been taught; one cannot conclude that the workers have absorbed, integrated, and learned it.

The degree to which group discussion is held concomitantly will determine the effectiveness of audio-visual aids as a primary technique in in-service training. As long as group discussion is held, and the often inordinate amount of time necessary to present movies or tape recordings reduced, then perhaps such aids can promote educational aims. In order to assume that such methods have an impact upon the learner, one must presuppose a high degree of motivation. For it is only the self-directing, goal-oriented, decisive learner who will and can learn from a movie, a poster board display, or a boring teacher or book. In a classroom in an academic setting there are, of course, such teachers and such teaching methods, but the dull thud of their impact is often offset by the fact that the student is at school to learn. While he may not be entirely well motivated, he has either paid tuition or contracted some fellowship arrangement involving his future. If he wants to learn he listens, takes notes, studies, asks questions, and generally applies himself to the task he has chosen to accomplish. Even if one were to assume that he didn't want to learn but only wanted to finish school and receive his degree, that student would still need to apply himself with a high degree of involvement so as to pass the course and become eligible for the degree. Even then, a student may tune out when the subject matter is over his head, too elementary, disorganized, or removed from his interests. It should be an axiom, although undoubtedly it is not, that where the subject matter fails to involve the student the teacher must, and where the teacher cannot entice him with the subject alone, ways of relating it to more stimulating material should be found.

The worker in an agency is not there primarily to learn, except to the extent necessary for him to keep his job and do it well. Naturally, a well motivated worker with intelligence and ambition will want to do his job as well as he can and therefore will try to learn as much as possible. Learning experience that does not sharpen his interest may easily be lost to him in training, thus the burden of communication may be even greater for the trainer in the agency than for the teacher in the school. Educational methods should rely upon staff participation; they should illustrate, elucidate, clarify. Unless visual aids are used to demonstrate a point just made or yet to be made through direct teaching or group discussion, they may serve as an intellectual resting place for the uninterested person and a manifest insult for the highly motivated, questioning learner.

The effectiveness of other reading material in the agency setting—whether policy manuals or professional literature—depends upon the worker's motivation and his realization that such reading is important to him in the carrying out of his job. This motivation can be stimulated by a supervisor or a colleague as well as by an exciting teacher in training sessions, but it is not to be assumed, in an agency any more than in a school, that literature will be read simply because it is there. One can rely very little on reading materials in in-service training, as their use will vary in accordance with individual capacities and interests. It cannot be emphasized too often that the role of a worker in an agency setting contains different expectations than does the role of a graduate student. Each invests himself in a different set of activities, and while learning is usually the primary aim of the student, it remains a secondary aim of the worker.

The objective of using educational methods in an inservice training program is to lead the workers to reflect on the meaning of their experiences and to gain increasing control over subsequent, structured experiences. Dewey often said that proper learning was a matter of learning the meaning of things, never things themselves. The responsibility of the teacher is to synthesize and organize facts or knowledge so that they may be integrated into life's practical realities. If the worker actively participates in this process through discussion and debate, he brings out his latent ideas and organizes his thinking so that he can use his knowledge. In order to argue, one must know something and order it logically. Even when attention is focused on one person in the training session, the rest of the group members will be thinking while he is speaking. As long as the teacher sustains a challenging level of discussion, for example through leading questions, there is seldom a loss in development while the group is grappling verbally with the content.

In a training session where the emphasis is placed erroneously upon narration or exposition of a subject rather than upon argument or discussion, it is not difficult to be impressed by the level and organization of the content. Yet the statement of a fact or a value hardly signifies its acceptance by the group, no matter how convincingly presented. Greater meanings are found when the workers are helped to explore the consequences of alternative solutions before the answers to the problems presented are provided by the teacher. Purposeful raising of questions leads out thought from memory, for such a process requires intellectual application by the person being taught.

What the teacher does with the group's answers is the essence of the educational process. Rather than respond in yes-or-no terms, he may introduce facts that will tend to support or invalidate answers. He may lead the workers through a process of thought to check the adequacy of the meanings they have drawn, or he may widen and enrich their conceptual activity by a range of information brought to bear on a problem. A word about the meaning and use of concepts might help to clarify this aspect of learning activity. According to the dictionary, a concept is "an idea representing the meaning of a universal term and comprehending the essential attributes of a class or logical species. An idea that includes all that is characteristically associated with, or suggested by, a term; a mental image of an action or thing; . . . an organized unity corresponding to some universal." [18]

Concepts as representatives of classes of "things" have educational value in that they reflect a stable, relatively permanent system of knowledge, a framework for thinking, and a set of abstractions that enable us to generalize. Usually labels are attached to concepts, but a label alone does not necessarily stand for a concept. The mindful behavior of a worker-in-training occurs after he deals first with things and then with names in the absence of things. His environment is enriched when names or abstractions derive from the classification of things, and when he has brought his mind to bear upon their significance and interrelationships.

Within the bureaucratic structure, the staff development process may be fitted into the existing balance of forces and personnel arrangements. The aims of training within an agency are always to be interpreted through the program screen of the agency, but the methods are borrowed from education. The content that is taught in in-service training and the activities of the nonprofessional social worker are necessarily limited in scope, but the way of teaching the material essential to the job is not very different from the methods used in formal education.

To the degree that public welfare staff are to be adequately prepared for social service tasks and direct work with their clientele, they must have more than rote teaching. As training succeeds in helping workers to respond conceptually, with limited knowledge but with self-direction within those limits, it will enable them to rise above the unrelated facts and grinding meaningless duties that all too often characterize public welfare operations. Even within the relatively inflexible structure of a government agency, informed decisions and creative actions can be encouraged, rather than rigid, unthinking, conforming habits.

This is the model of a public welfare worker that a well conceived and well executed agency training program can produce. In the absence of a graduate education in social work he would remain a nonprofessional, but his status and functioning, and his value to welfare clients and to the community at large, would be immeasurably enhanced.

Notes

Chapter One. Of People There Are Plenty

1. Wolfle, *America's Resources of Specialized Talent.*

2. Kahn, "Caseload Management: A Planned 'Package.'" (Mimeographed address, in preparation for publication.)

3. Wolfe, "Improving Services by Better Utilization of Staff," *Public Welfare,* XIX (April 1961), 53–62, 80–81.

4. Buell et al, "Reorganizing to Prevent and Control Disordered Behavior," *Mental Hygiene,* XLII (April 1958), 155–94.

5. Wolfle, *America's Resources of Specialized Talent,* p. 221. (Quotation used by permission of Harper & Row, Publishers.)

6. *Ibid.,* p. 171.

7. "Employment Projections to 1975," *Monthly Labor Review* LXXXVI (March 1963), 244–45.

8. Berengarten, *Admissions Prediction and Student Performance in Social Work Education,* p. 13.

9. National Social Welfare Assembly, *Salaries and Working Conditions of Social Welfare Manpower in 1960,* p. 56, table 30.

10. Baker, "Personnel in Social Work," in *Encyclopedia of Social Work,* p. 539.

11. "Statistics," in Lurie, ed., *Encyclopedia of Social Work,* p. 898, tables 42 and 43.

12. National Commission for Social Work Careers, *Annual Review,* 1965, p. 28.

13. French, *Needed Research on Social Work Manpower.*

14. Schorr, "Need for Trained Social Work Staff," *Social Security Bulletin,* XXIV (August 1961), 11–13.

15. U.S. Department of Health, Education, and Welfare, *Report of the Advisory Council on Child Welfare Services,* p. 42.

16. Winston, "The National Commitment to Eliminate Poverty," *Annual Review, National Commission for Social Work Careers,* February 1965, p. 6.

17. Schorr, "Need for Trained Social Work Staff," pp. 11–13.

18. Linford, "Education and In-Service Training for the Public Family and Children's Services," *Proceedings,* Council on Social Work Education, 1963, pp. 81–92.

19. U.S. Department of Health, Education, and Welfare, *Study of Staff Losses in Child Welfare and Family Service Agencies,* p. 25.

20. Linville, "Staffing Problems Under the New Service Amendments." *Public Welfare,* XXI (October 1963), 203.

21. Winston, "The National Commitment to Eliminate Poverty."

22. Osborn, Unpublished mimeographed memorandum, February 1961.

23. Venn, *Man, Education and Work,* pp. 70–71.

24. *Ibid.,* p. 139.

25. Meyer, "A Development Plan for Child Welfare Staff," *Children,* VIII (July–August 1961), 141–46.

26. Meyer, "Staff Development: A Social Work Process in a Public Child Welfare Agency," *Public Welfare,* XX (April 1962), 125.

Chapter Two. Public Welfare–Strains and Stresses

1. Vinter, "The Social Structure of Service," in Kahn, ed., *Issues in American Social Work,* p. 244.

2. Weissman and Baker, *Education for Social Workers in*

the Public Social Services, Vol. VII of Council on Social Work Education, *Social Work Curriculum Study.*

3. Council on Social Work Education, *Social Work Content in the Undergraduate Curriculum.*

4. Burns, "Future Social Security Policy and the APWA Leadership Role," *Public Welfare,* XXII (January 1964), 30.

5. U.S. Department of Health, Education, and Welfare, *Welfare in Review,* Statistical Supplement, 1964 Edition, tables 2 and 19.

6. Merriam, "Social Welfare Expenditures 1962–63," *Social Security Bulletin,* XXVI (November 1963), 8.

7. "Community Planning," *Public Welfare,* XXII (January 1964), 46–48.

8. Callison, "Federal Welfare Programs and Automation," in *Automation and Public Welfare,* Supplement to *Public Welfare* XXII (April 1964), 36.

9. De Schweinitz, *Interviewing in Social Security.*

10. Wilensky and Lebeaux, *Industrial Society and Social Welfare,* p. 153.

11. "Community Planning," *Public Welfare,* XXII (January 1964), 51–52.

12. Burns, "Future Social Security Policy," *Public Welfare,* XXII (January 1964), 29–32.

13. Burns, "What's Wrong with Public Welfare?" *Social Service Review,* XXXVI (June 1962), 115.

14. Hoshino, "The Means Test Can be Simplified." (Mimeographed address.)

15. Schwartz, "A Way to End the Means Test," *Social Work,* IX (July 1964), 3–12, 97.

16. Wilensky and Lebeaux, *Industrial Society and Social Welfare,* p. 294.

17. Vinter, "The Social Structure of Service," p. 257.

18. Merton, *Social Theory and Social Structure,* p. 123.

19. Stanley, *Professional Personnel for the City of New York,* p. 39.

20. *Ibid.,* p. 31.   21. *Ibid.,* p. 47.

22. Merton, "Bureaucratic Structure and Personality," in Merton, ed., *Social Theory and Social Structure,* p. 200.

23. Dimock, "Bureaucracy Self-Examined," in Merton, ed., *Reader in Bureaucracy,* p. 405.

24. Stanley, *Professional Personnel for the City of New York,* pp. 147–48.

25. *Ibid.,* pp. 135–36.   26. *Ibid.,* p. 136.

27. Mills, *The Sociological Imagination,* p. 93.

28. Stanley, *Professional Personnel for the City of New York,* p. 230.

29. Merton, "Bureaucratic Structure and Personality," pp. 195–206.

30. Richan, "A Theoretical Scheme for Determining Roles of Professional and Nonprofessional Personnel," *Social Work,* VI (October 1961), 22–28.

31. Finestone, "Some Specifics in Developing and Assessing a Staff Development Program." (Mimeographed address.)

32. Epstein, "Differential Use of Staff: A Method to Expand Social Services," *Social Work,* VII (October 1962), 66–72.

33. Heyman, "A Study of Effective Utilization of Social Workers in a Hospital Setting," *Social Work,* VI (October 1961), 36–43.

34. National Institute of Mental Health, "Pilot Study in Training Mental Health Counsellors," *American Journal of Orthopsychiatry,* XXXIII (July 1963), 678–89.

35. Weed and Denham, "Toward More Effective Use of the Nonprofessional Worker: A Recent Experiment," *Social Work,* VI (October 1961), 29–36.

36. Hamilton, "Editor's Page," *Social Work,* VII (January 1962), 2, 128.

37. Younghusband, *Training for Social Work,* p. 22.

38. The Oxford Universal Dictionary, Third Ed.

39. Dimock, "Bureacracy Self-Examined," pp. 397–98.

40. Blackey, *Group Leadership in Staff Training,* p. 20.

Chapter Three. Professionalism and Graduate Education

1. "Introduction," *The Professions, Daedalus,* XCII (Fall 1964), 651.

2. *Ibid.,* p. 652.

3. Carr-Saunders and Wilson, "Professions," *Encyclopedia of the Social Sciences,* XII, 480.

4. Goode, "Encroachment, Charletanism and the Emerging Professions: Psychology, Sociology, and Medicine," *American Sociological Review,* XXV (December 1960), 902.

5. *Ibid.,* p. 903. 6. *Ibid.,* p. 906.

7. Barbar, "Some Problems in the Sociology of the Professions," *The Professions, Daedalus,* p. 680.

8. Younghusband, *Training for Social Work,* pp. 122–23.

9. Whitehead, *Adventures of Ideas,* pp. 73–74.

10. Hughes, "The Professions," *The Professions, Daedalus,* p. 660.

11. Barbar, "Some Problems in the Sociology of the Professions," *The Professions, Daedalus,* p. 672.

12. Goode, "Encroachment, Charletanism and the Emerging Professions," p. 903.

13. Parsons, "The Professions and Social Structure," *Social Forces,* XVII (May 1939), 459.

14. Goode, "Community Within a Community—The Professions," *American Sociological Review,* XXII (April 1957), 195.

15. *Ibid.,* p. 196.

16. Brownell, "Foreword," in Blauch, ed., *Education for the Professions,* p. v.

17. Smalley, "Freedom and Necessity in Social Work Education," Council on Social Work Education, *Proceedings* (1963), pp. 59–60.

18. McGlothlin, *Patterns of Professional Education,* p. 72.

Chapter Four. The Staff Development Process

1. Meyer, "Staff Development: A Social Work Process in a Public Child Welfare Agency," *Public Welfare*, XX (April 1962), 126.

2. Younghusband, *Training for Social Work*, p. 134.

3. Dimock, "Bureaucracy Self-Examined," in Merton, ed., *Reader in Bureaucracy*, p. 399.

4. Blau, "Orientation Toward Clients in a Public Welfare Agency," *Administrative Science Quarterly*, V (December 1960), 341.

5. Merton, "Role of the Intellectual in Public Bureaucracy," in *Social Theory and Social Structure*, p. 216.

Chapter Five. Orientation and Training of Newly Hired Staff

1. Meyer, "A Development Plan for Child Welfare Staff," *Children*, VIII (July–August 1961), 141–46.

2. Merriam-Webster *New International Dictionary*, Unabridged, Second Ed.

Chapter Six. In-Service Training of Supervisors and Experienced Practitioners

1. Reynolds, *Learning and Teaching in the Practice of Social Work*, pp. 69–85.

Chapter Seven. Training Method

1. Merriam-Webster *New International Dictionary*, Unabridged, Second Ed.

2. *Ibid.*

3. Simon, "Decision-Making and Administrative Organization," in Merton, ed., *Reader in Bureaucracy*, p. 193.

4. Highet, *The Art of Teaching*, p. 11.

5. Vasey, "How Adequate and Flexible are the Legal Base and Social Policy which Underlie Family and Child Welfare Services and Resources?" in Cella and Lane, eds., *Basic Issues in Coordinating Family and Child Welfare Programs*, p. 47.

6. Shoben, "The Counsellor Theory as Personal Treatment," *Journal of Personnel and Guidance*, XL (1962), 617.

7. Hull, *Principles of Behavior*.

8. Miller and Dollard, *Social Learning and Imitation*.

9. Tolman, "The Determiners of Behavior at a Choice Point," *Psychological Review*, XLV (1938), 1–41.

10. Piaget, *Psychology of Intelligence*.

11. Reynolds, *Learning and Teaching in the Practice of Social Work*.

12. Towle, *The Learner in Education for the Professions*.

13. Hamilton, *Teaching Psychiatric Social Work*.

14. Robinson, *Supervision in Social Case Work*.

15. Dewey, *How We Think*.

16. McGlothlin, *Patterns of Professional Education*, p. 70.

17. Bode, *Modern Educational Theories*, p. 48.

18. Merriam-Webster *New International Dictionary*, Unabridged, Second Ed.

Bibliography

Abrahamson, Arthur C. *Group Methods in Supervision and Staff Development.* New York, Harper, 1959.

American Public Welfare Association (APWA). *Building Sound Staff Development.* Pamphlet No. II in Series on Services and Training. Chicago, APWA. 1958.

APWA Bienniel Round Table Conference, 1963. "The Great Step Forward in Public Welfare Services," *Public Welfare,* XXII, No. 1 (January 1964), 46–48.

—— "What's Behind Dependency?" *Public Welfare,* XXII, No. 1 (January 1964), 51–53.

APWA Committee on Social Work Education and Personnel. "Goals for Meeting Social Work Manpower Needs in Public Welfare Agencies," *Public Welfare,* XXI, No. 1 (January 1963), 2.

Baker, Mary R. "Personnel in Social Work," in Harry L. Lurie, ed., *Encyclopedia of Social Work.* New York, National Association of Social Workers (NASW), 1965. Vol. XV, pp. 532–40.

—— "How Effectively are We Utilizing Professional Staff Resources in Meeting Family and Child Welfare Needs?" in *Basic Issues in Coordinating Family and Child Welfare Programs.* Fels Institute Series. Philadelphia, University of Pennsylvania Press, 1964, pp. 95–117.

Barbar, Bernard. "Some Problems in the Sociology of the Professions," *Daedalus, The Professions.* Fall 1964, pp. 669–88.

Beck, Bertram M. "Job Definitions: A First Step," in *Education for Social Work.* (Proceedings, Council on Social Work Education. Eleventh Annual Program Meeting, Boston 1963.) New York, Council on Social Work Education, 1963.

Berengarten, Sidney. *Admissions Prediction and Student Performance in Social Work Education.* New York, Council on Social Work Education, 1964.

Bisno, Herbert. *The Place of the Undergraduate Curriculum in Social Work Education.* Vol. II of *Curriculum Study.* New York, Council on Social Work Education, 1959.

Blackey, Eileen A. *Group Leadership in Staff Training.* Washington, D.C., United States Department of Health, Education, and Welfare (USDHEW), 1957. Bureau of Public Assistance Report 29 or Children's Bureau Publication 361–1957.

Blau, Peter M. "Orientation Toward Clients in a Public Welfare Agency," *Administrative Science Quarterly,* V, No. 3 (December 1960), 341–61.

Blau, Peter M., and W. Richard Scott. *Formal Organizations: A Comparative Approach.* San Francisco, Chandler Publishing Company, 1962.

Bode, Boyd Henry. *Modern Educational Theories.* New York, Macmillan, 1927. (New York, Vintage.)

Boehm, Werner W., dir. and coord. *Curriculum Study.* New York, Council on Social Work Education, 1959. Vols. II and VII.

Boehm, Werner W. "Diagnostic Categories in Social Casework," in *Social Work Practice, 1962.* (Published for the National Conference of Social Welfare.) New York, Columbia University Press, 1962, pp. 3–26.

Bratton, Willie V. "Report of Study of Utilization of Auxiliary Personnel Assigned to Social Service Staff in Public and Voluntary Social Agencies." Washington, D.C., USDHEW, mimeographed, *ca.* 1963.

Brieland, Donald. *Differential Use of Manpower for Foster Care in a Public Child Welfare Program*. Springfield, Illinois Department of Child and Family Services, June 1964.

Brownell, Samuel. "Foreword" in Lloyd E. Blauch, ed., *Education for the Professions*. Washington, D.C. USDHEW, Office of Education, 1955.

Buell, Bradley. *Community Planning for Human Services*. New York, Columbia University Press, 1952.

Buell, Bradley, et al. "Reorganizing to Prevent and Control Disordered Behavior," *Mental Hygiene*, XLII (April 1958), 155–94.

Bureau of Family Services. *Characteristics of State Public Assistance Plans Under the Social Security Act: Staff Development Provisions*. Washington, D.C., USDHEW, 1964. Public Assistance Report 51.

—— *Report of the Cooperative Project on Public Welfare Staff Training*. Washington, D.C., USDHEW, 1963. Vols. I and II.

Bureau of Public Assistance, Division of Technical Training, *Compilation of Working Papers on the Educational Standards Project*. Washington, D.C., USDHEW, October 1960.

Burns, Eveline M. "Future Social Security Policy and the APWA Leadership Role." (APWA Bienniel Round Table Conference, 1963.) *Public Welfare*, XXII, No. 1 (January 1964), 29–32.

—— "What's Wrong With Public Welfare?" *Social Service Review*, XXXVI, No. 2 (June 1962), 111–22.

Callison, James. "Federal Welfare Programs and Automation: An Overview," in *Automation and Public Welfare* (Supplement to *Public Welfare*, XXII, No. 2, April 1964), pp. 33–35.

Carr-Saunders, A. M., and P. A. Wilson. "Professions," in *Encyclopedia of the Social Sciences*. New York, Macmillan, 1933. Vol. XII, pp. 476–80.

Cella, Charles P., Jr., and Rodney P. Lane, eds. *Basic Issues in Coordinating Family and Child Welfare Programs*. Fels

Institute Series. Philadelphia, University of Pennsylvania Press, 1964.

Cooper, E. Myles. "Research on Standards for Caseworker Functions," *Public Welfare*, XIX, No. 2 (April 1961), 58–62.

Council on Social Work Education (CSWE). *Curriculum Study.* See Boehm.

—— *Memorandum on Implications for Social Work Curriculum of Community Research Associates' Material.* (Prepared for the Louis W. and Maud Hill Family Foundation, St. Paul.) Mimeographed pamphlet, 1960.

—— *Social Work Content in the Undergraduate Curriculum.* New York, CSWE, 1962.

—— *Statistics on Social Work Education.* (November 1, 1963 and Academic Year 1962–63.) New York, CSWE, 1963.

Daedalus. (Journal of the American Academy of Arts and Sciences.) Fall 1964 issue, *The Professions.*

De Schweinitz, Elizabeth and Karl. *Interviewing in Social Security.* Washington, D.C., USDHEW, Social Security Administration, Bureau of Old-Age and Survivors Insurance, 1961.

Dewey, John. *How We Think.* Boston, Heath, 1933.

Dimock, Marshall E. "Bureaucracy Self-Examined," in Robert K. Merton, ed., *Social Theory and Social Structure.* New York, Free Press, 1957.

Encyclopedia of Social Work. See Lurie, ed.

Epstein, Laura. "Differential Use of Staff: A Method to Expand Social Services," *Social Work*, VII, No. 4 (October 1962), 66–72.

Fenton, Norman, and Kermit T. Wiltse. *Group Methods in the Public Welfare Program.* Palo Alto, Calif., Pacific Books, 1963.

Finestone, Samuel. "Issues Involved in Developing Diagnostic Classifications for Casework: An Outline of Current Trends," in *1960 Casework Papers.* New York, Family Service Association of America, pp. 139–54.

―――― "Differential Utilization of Casework Staff in Public Welfare: Major Dimensions." Mimeographed paper, May 1964.

―――― "Some Observations on Treatment Classifications in Social Casework." Unpublished paper, 1962.

―――― "Some Specifics in Developing and Assessing a Staff Development Program." Mimeographed address, 1964.

French, David G. *Needed Research on Social Work Manpower: With Particular Reference to Program Areas for which the Federal Government has Responsibility.* (Report to the Task Force on Social Work Education and Manpower.) Washington, D.C., USDHEW, Welfare Administration, Bureau of Family Services, 1964.

French, David G., and Alex Rosen. "Personnel Entering Social Work Employment from Schools of Social Work, 1957," *Social Work Education* (Special Recruitment Issue), VI, No. 2 (April 1958), 9–17.

Goode, William J. "Community Within a Community: The Professions," *American Sociological Review*, XXII, No. 2 (April 1957), 194–200.

―――― "Encroachment, Charlatanism and the Emerging Professions: Psychology, Sociology, and Medicine," *American Sociological Review*, XXV, No. 6 (December 1960), 902–14.

Greenwood, Ernest. "Attributes of a Profession," *Social Work*, II, No. 3 (July 1957), 45–55.

Hamilton, Gordon. "Editor's Page," *Social Work*, VII, No. 1 (January 1962), 2, 128.

―――― *Teaching Psychiatric Social Work.* (Proceedings of the Institute on Teaching Psychiatric Social Work, Atlantic City, May 1955.) New York, NASW, Psychiatric Social Work Section.

Heyman, Margaret M. "Criteria for the Allocation of Cases According to Levels of Staff Skill," *Social Casework*, XLII, No. 7 (July 1961), 325–31.

———— "A Study of Effective Utilization of Social Workers in a Hospital Setting," *Social Work*, VI, No. 2 (April 1961), 36–43.

Hoshino, George. "The Means Test Can Be Simplified." (Address delivered at the 91st Annual Forum, National Conference on Social Welfare, Los Angeles, May 1964.) Mimeographed.

Hughes, Everett C. "The Professions," *Daedalus, The Professions*, XCII, No. 4 (Fall 1964), 659–68.

Hull, Clark L. *Principles of Behavior: An Introduction to Behavior Theory*. New York, Appleton, 1943.

Kahn, Alfred J. "Caseload Management: A Planned 'Package,'" in his unpublished collected papers, New York, Columbia University School of Social Work, 1962.

Linford, Alton A. "Education and In-Service Training for the Public Family and Children's Services," in *Proceedings, Council on Social Work Education*. New York, cswe, 1963, 81–92.

Linville, Clyde W., Jr. "Staffing Problems Under the New Service Amendments," *Public Welfare*, XXI, No. 4 (October 1963), 201–4, 226–27.

Litwak, Eugene. "Models of Bureaucracy which Permit Conflict," *American Journal of Sociology*, LXVIII, No. 2 (September 1961), 177–84.

Lurie, Harry L., ed. *Encyclopedia of Social Work*. New York, National Association of Social Workers, 1965.

McGlothlin, William J. *Patterns of Professional Education*. New York, Putnam, 1960.

Merton, Robert K. "Bureaucratic Structure and Personality," in *Social Theory and Social Structure*. New York, Free Press, 1957, pp. 195–206. Rev. ed.

———— "Role of the Intellectual in Public Bureaucracy," in *Social Theory and Social Structure*. New York, Free Press, 1957, pp. 207–24. Rev. ed.

Merton, Robert K., et al., eds. *Reader in Bureaucracy*. New York, Free Press, 1952.

Merton, Robert K., George G. Reader, and Patricia Kendall, eds. *The Student Physician*, Cambridge, Harvard University Press, 1957.

Meyer, Carol H. "A Development Program for Child Welfare Staff," *Children*, VIII, No. 4 (July–August 1961), 141–46.

—— "Staff Development: A Social Work Process in a Public Child Welfare Agency," *Public Welfare*, XX, No. 2 (April 1962), 125–31.

Miller, Neal Elgar, and John Dollard. *Social Learning and Imitation*. (Published for the Institute of Human Relations.) New Haven, Yale University Press, 1941.

Mills, C. Wright. *The Sociological Imagination*. New York, Grove Press, 1961.

Monahan, Fergus Thomas. *A Study of Nonprofessional Personnel in Social Work—the Army Social Work Specialist*. Washington, D.C., Catholic University of America Press, 1960.

Moscrop, Martha. *In-Service Training for Social Agency Practice*. Toronto, University of Toronto Press, 1958.

National Association of Social Workers. *Utilization of Personnel in Social Work: Those with Full Professional Education and those without*. (Final Report, 1961.) New York, NASW, 1962, mimeographed.

National Commission for Social Work Careers. *Annual Review*, 1965.

National Institute of Mental Health. "Pilot Study in Training Mental Health Counselors," *American Journal of Orthopsychiatry*, XXXIII, No. 4 (July 1963), 678–79.

National Social Welfare Assembly and U.S. Dept. of Labor, Bureau of Labor Statistics. *Salaries and Working Conditions of Social Welfare Manpower in 1960*. New York, National Social Welfare Assembly, 1961.

Oettinger, Katherine B. "Public Child Welfare Manpower Needs," *Public Welfare*, XX, No. 3 (July 1962), 151–54.

Osborn, Phyllis. Unpublished mimeographed memorandum, February 1961.

Parsons, Talcott. *The Social System.* New York, Free Press, 1952.

—— "The Professions and Social Structure," *Social Forces*, XVII, No. 4 (May 1939), 457–67.

Piaget, Jean. *The Psychology of Intelligence.* Malcolm Percy and D. E. Berlyne, tr. New York, Harcourt, 1950.

Polansky, Norman A. "The Professional Identity in Social Work," in Alfred J. Kahn. ed., *Issues in American Social Work.* New York, Columbia University Press, 1959, pp. 293–318.

Reissman, Leonard. "A Study of Role Conceptions in Bureaucracy," *Social Forces*, XXVII, No. 3 (March 1949), 30–310.

Reynolds, Bertha. *Learning and Teaching in the Practice of Social Work.* New York, Rinehart, 1942.

Richan, Willard C., ed. *Utilization of Personnel in Social Work: Those with Full Professional Education and those without.* See National Association of Social Workers.

—— "A Theoretical Scheme for Determining Roles of Professional and Nonprofessional Personnel," *Social Work*, VI, No. 4 (October 1961), 22–28.

Rioch, Elkes, Flint, Usdansky, Newman and Silber. "NIMH Pilot Study in Training Mental Health Counselors," *American Journal of Orthopsychiatry*, XXXIII, No. 4 (July 1963), 678–89.

Robinson, Virginia. *Supervision in Social Case Work.* Chapel Hill, University of North Carolina Press, 1936.

—— *Training for Skill in Social Case Work.* Philadelphia, University of Pennsylvania Press, 1942.

Romanyshyn, John M. "The Undergraduate Social Welfare Sequence," *Public Welfare*, XXII, No. 3 (July 1964), 202–6.

Schorr, Alvin L. "Need For Trained Social Work Staff: A Ten-

Year Goal," *Social Security Bulletin*, XXIV, No. 8 (August 1961), 11–13.

Schwartz, Edward E. "A Way to End the Means Test," *Social Work*, IX, No. 3 (July 1964), 3–12, 97.

Shoben, Edward J. "The Counsellor Theory as Personal Treatment," *Journal of Personnel and Guidance*, XL (1962), 617.

Simon, Herbert A. *Administrative Behavior*. New York, Macmillan, 1957. Rev. ed.

—— "Decision-Making and Administrative Organization," in Merton et al., eds., *Reader in Bureaucracy*. New York, Free Press, 1952, pp. 185–94.

Smalley, Ruth E. "Freedom and Necessity in Social Work Education," in *Education for Social Work*. (Proceedings of Eleventh Annual Program Meeting, Council on Social Work Education, Boston.) New York, CSWE, 1963, pp. 54–65.

Stanley, David T., et al. *Professional Personnel for the City of New York*. Washington, D.C., Brookings Institution, 1963.

Stone, Olive, Florence Aitchinson, and Cynthia Nathan. *Utilization of Staff with Different Levels of Education, and Illustrative Selected Local and State Job Specifications*. Washington, D.C., USDHEW, Bureau of Family Services.

Tannar, Virginia L. *Selected Social Work Concepts for Public Welfare Workers*. Washington, D.C., USDHEW, Welfare Administration, Bureau of Family Services, 1964.

Tebow, Hilda P. *Staff Development as an Integral Part of Administration*. Washington, D.C., USDHEW, Bureau of Family Services, 1959. Public Assistance Report 35.

Thomas, Edwin J., Donna L. McLeod, et al. *In-Service Training and Reduced Workloads*. New York, Russell Sage Foundation, 1960.

Tollen, William B. *Study of Staff Losses in Child Welfare and Family Service Agencies*. See USDHEW.

Tolman, R. S. "The Determiners of Behavior at a Choice Point," *Psychological Review*, XLV (1938), 1–41.

Towle, Charlotte. *The Case Method in Teaching Social Work.* (Proceedings of the Institute on the Use of the Case Method in Teaching Psychiatric Social Work, Atlantic City, 1959.) New York, National Association of Social Workers, 1959.

────── *The Learner in Education for the Professions as Seen in Education for Social Work.* Chicago, University of Chicago Press, 1954.

────── *Some Reflections on Social Work Education.* London, Family Welfare Association, 1956.

United Nations. *In-Service Training in Social Welfare.* New York, United Nations, 1952. UN Sales No. 1952.IV.9.

U.S. Dept. of Health, Education, and Welfare (USDHEW). *New Directions in Health, Education, and Welfare.* (Background Papers on Current and Emerging Issues.) Washington, D.C., USDHEW, Office of the Secretary, 1963.

────── *Public Social Welfare Personnel.* Washington, D.C., USDHEW, Welfare Administration, Bureau of Family Services and Children's Bureau. 1962.

────── *Report of the U.S. Advisory Council on Child Welfare Services.* Washington, D.C., USDHEW, Social Security Administration, Children's Bureau, December 28, 1959.

────── *Staff Development in Public Welfare Agencies.* Washington, D.C., USDHEW, Welfare Administration, Bureau of Family Services and Children's Bureau, 1963.

────── *Study of Staff Losses in Child Welfare and Family Service Agencies.* Washington, D.C., USDHEW, Social Security Administration, Children's Bureau, 1960. Publication 383.

────── *Training for Service in Public Assistance.* Washington, D.C., USDHEW, Social Security Administration, Bureau of Public Assistance and Bureau of Family Services, 1961.

────── *Welfare in Review, Statistical Supplement, 1964 Edition,* tables 2 and 19.

U.S. Dept. of Labor, Bureau of Labor Statistics. "Employment Projections to 1975," *Monthly Labor Review,* LXXXVI, No. 3 (March 1963), 240–48.

Vasey, Wayne. "How Adequate and Flexible are the Legal Base and Social Policy which Underlie Family and Child Welfare Services and Resources?" in Charles P. Cella, Jr. and Rodney P. Lane, eds., *Basic Issues in Coordinating Family and Child Welfare Programs*. Fels Institute Series. Philadelphia, University of Pennsylvania Press, 1964, pp. 44–59.

Venn, Grant. *Man, Education and Work*. Washington, D.C., American Council on Education, 1964.

Vinter, Robert D. "The Social Structure of Service," in Alfred J. Kahn, ed., *Issues in American Social Work*. New York, Columbia University Press, 1959, pp. 242–69.

Weber, Max. *The Theory of Social and Economic Organization*. A. M. Henderson and Talcott Parsons, tr., Talcott Parsons, ed. New York, Oxford University Press, 1947.

—— "The Essentials of Bureaucratic Organization: An Ideal-Type Construction," in Herman D. Stein and Richard A. Howard, eds., *Social Perspectives on Behavior*. New York, Free Press, 1958, pp. 564–71.

Weed, Verne, and William H. Denham. "Toward More Effective Use of the Nonprofessional Worker: A Recent Experiment," *Social Work*, VI, No. 4 (October 1961), 29–36.

Weisbrod, Helen J. "A Guide for Administrative Planning of Staff Development Responsibilities," *Public Welfare*, XX, No. 3 (July 1962), 168–69.

Weissman, Irving, and Mary R. Baker. *Education for Social Workers in the Public Social Services*. Vol. VII of *Curriculum Study*. New York, Council on Social Work Education, 1959.

Weller, Evalyn G., Martha Moscrop, Mrs. Freda F. Burnside. *Building Sound Staff Development*. See American Public Welfare Association.

Whitehead, Alfred North. *Adventures of Ideas*. New York, Macmillan, 1933. (New York, Mentor.)

Wilensky, Harold L., and Charles N. Lebeaux. *Industrial So-*

ciety and Social Welfare. New York, Russell Sage Foundation, 1958.

Williamson, Margaret. *Supervision—Principles and Methods.* New York, Woman's Press, 1950.

Winston, Ellen. "The National Commitment to Eliminate Poverty: A Challenge to Social Welfare, Education and Manpower," *Annual Review 1965*(National Commission for Social Work Careers), pp. 6, 26.

—— "Public Welfare's Dilemma," *Public Welfare*, XIX, No. 3 (July 1961), pp. 93–94, 126.

Witte, Ernest F. "Training Social Work Associates," in *Proceedings, Eleventh Annual Program Meeting, Council on Social Work Education.* New York, CSWE, 1963, pp. 12–24.

Wittman, Milton. "Utilization of Personnel with Various Levels of Training: Implications for Professional Development." (Paper presented at Tenth Anniversary Symposium, NASW, Atlantic City, May 22, 1965.) Unpublished.

Wolfe, Corinne H. "Staff Development—Administrative Framework and Attendant Responsibilities in a Public Welfare Agency." Mimeographed paper, 1964.

—— "Improving Services by Better Utilization of Staff," *Public Welfare*, XIX, No. 2 (April 1961), 53–57, 80–81.

Wolfle, Dael. *America's Resources of Specialized Talent.* New York, Harper, 1954.

Younghusband, Eileen L., ed. *Report of the Working Party on Social Workers in the Local Authority Health and Welfare Services.* London, Ministry of Health, 1959.

Younghusband, Eileen L. *Training for Social Work: Third International Survey.* United Nations Dept. of Economic and Social Affairs. New York, United Nations, 1958.

—— "Staffing Public Welfare Services," *Public Welfare*, XXI, No. 3 (July 1963), 115–18, 147–48.